# Mahboba's Promise

# Mahboba's Promise

HOW ONE WOMAN MADE A WORLD OF DIFFERENCE

## MAHBOBA RAWI
WITH VANESSA MICKAN-GRAMAZIO

BANTAM
SYDNEY • AUCKLAND • TORONTO • NEW YORK • LONDON

Some of the names of people in this book have
been changed in the interests of their privacy.

MAHBOBA'S PROMISE
A BANTAM BOOK

First published in Australia and New Zealand in 2005
by Bantam

National Library of Australia
Cataloguing-in-Publication Entry

Rawi, Mahboba.
Mahboba's promise.

ISBN 1 86325 429 3.

1. Rawi, Mahboba.  2. Refugees - Australia - Biography.  3.
Afghans - Australia - Biography.  I. Mickan-Gramazio, Vanessa. II. Title.

325.21092

Transworld Publishers,
a division of Random House Australia Pty Ltd
20 Alfred Street, Milsons Point, NSW 2061
http://www.randomhouse.com.au

Random House New Zealand Limited
18 Poland Road, Glenfield, Auckland

Transworld Publishers,
a division of The Random House Group Ltd
61-63 Uxbridge Road, Ealing, London W5 5SA

Random House Inc
1745 Broadway, New York, New York 10036

Cover photo by Lisa D'Ambra
In photo section: photos pp. 3,4,5 (top) and 7 (below) by Lisa D'Ambra
Typeset by Midland Typesetters in Berling Roman 12/17.5pt, Maryborough, Victoria
Printed and bound by Griffin Press, Netley, South Australia

10 9 8 7 6 5 4 3 2 1

**Mahboba Rawi** was born in Kabul, Afghanistan, and escaped as a teenager in 1982 when her country was under Soviet occupation. After living as a refugee in Pakistan and India she moved to Australia in 1984. She is the founder and President of Mahboba's Promise, a charity that supports widows and orphans in Afghanistan and the refugee camps of Pakistan. She lives in Sydney with her two children and her husband.

**Vanessa Mickan-Gramazio** was born in Brisbane in 1969. She has worked for major publishing houses as a book editor for the past ten years, and has a Masters in Writing. She lives in Sydney with her husband.

*This book is dedicated to*
*Tamana and Sourosh*
*and all the children of Afghanistan*

# Prologue

The Kabul I knew is gone. I drive along the streets of the city and I can't recognise anything. Where there were crowded shops and restaurants there is a deserted street of bombed-out buildings. Houses and gardens that were once filled with flowers and fruit trees have been reduced to dust. I see families sheltering in destroyed buildings; they haven't got any water or electricity or sewerage. Children are picking through the garbage that lies by the side of the road, looking for something to eat. I didn't know it was possible for a town to change so much in twenty years.

I stop near a crowded bazaar and get out of the car. I see a little girl, only seven years old or so, standing alone among the stalls. Her neck is stooped, weighed down by a heavy basket hanging around her neck on a string. It's filled with chewing gum, packets of biscuits and chocolate bars that she's trying to sell. The basket is old and all the goods inside are covered in dust. The girl's face is dusty, too, and her hair is matted. It looks like it hasn't been washed for quite a while. Beneath the dust there is a pretty face, with big dark brown innocent eyes. She is very thin, her clothes don't match and she hasn't got any shoes.

I walk over and ask her what her name is. 'Khatera,' she says, a little scared to talk to me. I notice that her neck looks red, and bend down to look closely. The skin is grazed and raw from where the string has cut into her skin. My heart burns when I see the marks. She looks about the same age as my son back home in Australia, who is probably in his nice clean pyjamas in bed right now.

I take Khatera's hand – it is so tiny and thin – and ask her where she lives. She tells me she lives nearby with her mother and little brother and sister. I give her enough money to buy some food for her and her family, give her the address of my uncle's house, where I am staying while I am visiting Kabul, and ask her if she will come and see me with her mother the next morning. She nods.

~

Khatera's mother has big dark circles under her eyes that show she has been through a lot. Like Khatera, she's terribly thin. I ask her how much Khatera earns each month in the bazaar, and she says about five hundred Afghanis, a little over ten Australian dollars.

'If I was able to give you three times what Khatera makes would you let her go to school and stop her from going out to work on the street?' I ask.

She starts crying and says, 'You feel sorry for my daughter – how do you think I feel? I see her neck cut and sore, but there's nothing I can do. My husband has been killed and I've got a son and daughter younger than her at home. She's the only one in the family who can provide for us.' She says that Khatera makes enough each day to buy bread for the family. They live on bread and black tea. She worries every day about what might happen to Khatera – a little girl like her out on the street on her own.

I start to cry, too. Khatera's mother can't believe that a stranger would offer her money to feed her family. No-one has ever helped them before. But how can I turn my back when this tiny girl has to support her whole family? I tell her that if Khatera goes to school I will make sure that once a month there will be 1,500 Afghanis – or about fifty Australian dollars, just under the average monthly wage in Afghanistan – waiting for her at my uncle's house, for as long as she wants it. It is my promise to her. And her promise to me is that Khatera will never go out to sell things at the bazaar again.

I take the biscuits, chewing gum and chocolate bars out of Khatera's basket, put them in a plastic bag and hand them back to her, and throw away the basket. I say, 'From today you're not going out on the street any more.'

The joy I get out of seeing the happiness on her face will be enough to last me the rest of my life. It is so beautiful to have been able to stop her from what she was doing. In my language, 'Khatera' means memory. I hug Khatera and tell her, 'You will stay in my memory forever.'

# Chapter 1

The moment my father first saw my mother, Gulshan, he knew he wanted to marry her. He was little more than a boy, only fifteen. She was a girl of twelve, and very beautiful. He spotted her walking through a tiny village called Abdara when he was on holidays in Panjshir Valley, two and a half hours' drive from his home in Kabul.

To my eyes, Panjshir Valley is as beautiful as the Swiss Alps. The Panjshir River is sparkling and green, the mountains are jagged and capped with snow and, unlike many parts of Afghanistan, there are plenty of trees. In my mother's time, life there was gentle. There were no shops; people grew their own food and cooked their own bread each day.

Like all the girls in her village, my mother never went to school. And when she was a girl she didn't cover her face with the *burqa*, as women and girls usually did in the city in those days. The girls just covered their hair with their scarves and left their faces bare because the village was so small everyone knew each other. Men and women worked in the fields together and joked with each other. The faces of the people in that village looked as pure as those of children from the city.

Her father died when she was very young, so she and her brother and sister were brought up singlehandedly by my grandmother, Janat Bagum. My grandmother had to work like a man. She supported her children by growing grapes and other fruit. So she could protect the fruit from thieves at night she would take her mattress and blanket and sleep in the orchard. She wasn't scared of thieves or snakes; she wasn't scared of anything. Even when the Russians came years later and everybody went to hide in the mountains from their warplanes and bombs, she refused to go.

My father, Ali Ahmed, was brought up in Kabul and had a totally different childhood – a city childhood. His father, Walee Mohammed, was born in Abdara then moved to Kabul, but never enjoyed city life. He owned a house in Panjshir Valley and travelled there often. My father went with him for holidays, and that was how he came to see my mother that day.

It was against our culture for a man to approach a woman directly so my father approached my grandmother to ask for my mother's hand. If someone from the city comes and proposes to a village woman, it's an honour for the family to say yes. My grandmother agreed and they were engaged. My father returned to Kabul for a few months and then returned to marry her. After the wedding they put my mother on a horse for the first time in her life and she and my father set out for Kabul, a place she had only heard of. She was very young, so they would have to wait a while before starting their real married life.

My father was a hat maker when he got married to my mum. He worked hard but he was poor. My mother soon found out that as a married woman in Kabul she was now poorer than the people in her village. At least in the village she had milk from the cows every day, fruit from the trees, water from the mountain springs, and wheat and corn from the fields. In Kabul, if you didn't have money, you didn't have food. But she was a wise girl and she learned quickly and coped with the new way of life in the city, making a comfortable home for her and my father. Then when she was about fourteen she became pregnant with my brother Anwar. Two more boys, Omar and Assad, followed.

My mother didn't have an easy time when she was carrying me, her fourth child. Seven months into the pregnancy she went for a holiday in Abdara and became very sick. She had eaten something that had poisoned her. She rushed back to Kabul and went into hospital, where they pumped out her stomach.

She carried me to full term but I was very tiny. My mother says I was the size of her hand. I was so small she couldn't put clothes on me; she had to wrap me in cloth. My mother had a midwife to help her, but there was no machine to help me breathe. It was difficult for my mother, but a great aunt on my father's side, who I grew up to call Grandma, helped out by feeding and changing me. She was like a second mother to me. Even though she was an old woman, she fed me from her breast. Nothing came out; she just wanted to comfort me. One of my father's brothers, Uncle Haji, was like a second father to me. He knew my mother had a lot of work to do cooking and cleaning so he would say, look after your work and I will look after Mahboba. So I had a lot of love as I grew up.

My father was no longer a poor man; he was working at our country's version of parliament house as a secretary. One of his brothers-in-law had worked in the government and had helped him to get a junior government job some years before, and my father had worked his way up. We lived in a nice suburb called Shahr-e-now, where many government staff lived. You were considered fortunate to live in Shahr-e-now. It had the best schools, paved roads like here in Australia, big houses, parks, a cinema and restaurants. The houses had wonderful gardens filled with all kinds of flowers and apple trees and vegetable patches.

We had a three-storey house. Downstairs was the kitchen, bathroom and the visitors room: in every Afghani house there is one room that is only used when someone comes to visit or stay over. The top storey was my father's and we weren't allowed up there – except sometimes to go and clean. We slept on the second storey in one big room, my mother and all the children together. Even middle-class families like us didn't have beds. We all slept on the floor on thin cotton mattresses that could be folded away during the day.

Our house was one of four owned by my father and his three brothers. My grandfather, Walee Mohammed, had owned a big piece of land and given it to his sons. At first they all lived with their mother and sisters in one house, then when they could afford to, they each added a house until it became like a group of townhouses.

People in Afghanistan have big families. Each of my father's brothers had between five and nine children, and every two years or so my mother would have another baby. My sister Zarmina was born, followed by another three brothers – Sidiq, Abdullah and Yama – so there were almost thirty kids to hang out with every day. We were never lonely. Every day we played and ate and went to school together. My father's three sisters each had eight or nine children. The sisters had moved away when they married, but every Thursday night they would come over with their husbands and children for a get-together. Friday was the one day off each week, for rest and for prayer.

In Afghani culture, when there's a party the kids are expected to go outside, so my cousins and I would go into the yard and play hide-and-seek or a game like hopscotch. Sometimes we'd make a man from earth and water and leave it to dry. You had to be creative because there were very few toys available. Some of the boys had bicycles or balls, but if you were a girl there was nothing, except handmade dolls. It took a woman several weeks to sew a doll, so you were very lucky to get one. Because I was so small when I was born, and the first girl after three boys, everyone gave me a lot of attention and I always had a doll. As soon as I lost one or it wore out I got another one.

When my mother and aunts had finished cooking we'd go inside to help serve dinner. We would lay a long white tablecloth on the floor. The adults would sit and we would bring in platters of lovely smelling, delicious-looking food for them. Rice with sultanas and carrot, handmade pastries stuffed with garlic leaves, lamb and chicken cooked in Afghani spices, soups, flat bread; and then for dessert, fruit and different kinds of sweet milk puddings. We wanted to go and just grab the food, but adults always ate before children. All Afghan girls and boys are taught to respect adults.

One of the older female cousins would take all the kids who were under twelve into another room, but a few children, the ones who never made a mess or who were the favourites, would be allowed to stay. I got to stay sometimes, and I would feel like a queen. All the other kids would be jealous because they had to wait and eat the leftovers. Of course my mother and aunties would always make plenty of food so that there would be enough.

I never once saw my mother sit with the adults to eat. She was always standing somewhere to the side serving people food and making sure they were happy. In Afghani society hospitality is one of the greatest virtues and it is particularly important that a wife be welcoming and show her guests hospitality. She cooked beautifully, and always in the old way. My father had a modern kitchen installed for her but she never touched the new stove or sink or benches.

On the floor she built her own traditional wood oven out of bricks. She would sit on the kitchen floor preparing food, cooking on the stove and even doing the dishes in a big tub.

My mother was still very much a village woman. She didn't want to wear make-up or sleeveless dresses. As soon as she left her village and came to the city she wore a *burqa*, which covers you from head to toe, whenever she left the house.

When I lost my first baby tooth my parents sent me to school. That was how most parents in Afghanistan knew when to send their kids to school. Afghani people don't place a lot of importance on paperwork or dates. We didn't have birth certificates, and didn't celebrate birthdays because it is not a Muslim tradition. My parents didn't know exactly when any of us were born. My mother says that I was born around New Year's Eve – but she doesn't know which year. Baby teeth usually start to fall out when you're six or seven so I guess that's how old I was when I started school.

My parents wanted me to have a modern education and upbringing. Sometimes I wonder if my father sensed that everything was about to change in our country and that I needed to be prepared. Sometimes he took me to do the shopping with him, and for an Afghani father that was a bit strange. Fathers took their sons, to teach them how to look after the women, whose role was to stay at home and do the housework. He would get ready for work, ask my mother what she needed, and take me on the twenty-minute walk to the shop. On the way he would tell me, 'You are like a boy.

You are loyal, and brave like a lion. Always stand on your own two feet.' He told me to listen to how he dealt with the shopkeepers, so I would learn. Then he would go off to work and I would walk home alone with the shopping – meat, vegetables and lemons, maybe some rice. At first I was scared of somebody taking the shopping from me, so I would clutch it to my chest, but after a while I learnt to be brave.

He didn't take me because there were no boys in the family to do it; he took me because he wanted to teach me. And I always paid attention to my father. Everybody did. In Afghanistan there is usually one man in each family who has authority and who everyone asks to sort out disputes or give advice. As my grandfather was always out working hard, and travelling to Panjshir Valley when he had a chance, the job ending up falling to my father.

From an early age he supported his brothers and sisters, made sure they got an education and helped them find jobs. Then when they married and had children he became responsible for the whole extended family, all my aunts and cousins. He was like a father to everybody, and a figure of authority. If the young boys skipped school he'd ride off on his bicycle to find them and lock them up in their house for a couple of hours to teach them a lesson. When a couple was having marriage problems, or members of the family weren't getting on with each other, they called on him to help find a solution. If he caught someone in the family drinking alcohol, or if he found out that a husband had hit his wife, he punished them with a beating. There was no such thing as marriage counselling and a woman wouldn't even bother to ring the police if her husband was hitting her, so he was playing a necessary role and people respected him. When he entered someone's house they usually chose a high place for him to sit. While he was talking, they listened to him with their eyes cast down. And when he told them to do something, they followed his rule.

My father was strict at home, and taught me a lot. Like the importance of giving to other people. Because he worked with the government, he had a lot of contacts with people who could make things happen. In Kabul at that time there were many educated people – writers, teachers, doctors and others with high-level qualifications – competing for jobs. People from the rural areas had no education and found it hard to get work in the city so my father helped them to find jobs as security guards, airport staff or clerks. He helped a lot of orphans from my mother's village in Panjshir Valley to get jobs, and provided financial support for my mother's side of the family.

Being a provider for his brothers and sisters, he didn't have much chance for an education himself; the way he worked his way up to a high position was by showing the utmost honesty. He had access to government ministers and many people in his position were tempted to take bribes in exchange for a minister's signature on a document. My father wasn't, and that's why his bosses liked him. Honesty wasn't always a popular trait, though. If he disliked a person or disagreed with something they'd done he'd always try to tell them to their face rather than criticise them behind their back, and that made some people wary of him. It was as if he would sooner die than be dishonest.

Bribes were never going to be a temptation to my father because he was never greedy for money. We were quite well off by Afghani standards. My father owned two houses in Kabul, but he wasn't interested in leading a flashy lifestyle. Even when he had money he didn't buy a car, he just kept riding his bicycle. He always said that he didn't want to forget where he had come from.

One of my happiest memories of my father is when I was little and every night he would come home from work with an apple for each of us. Then he'd play with me and my younger brothers and sister, and carry us around on his shoulders. At times like this he brought so much joy. He could be funny and make you laugh so much you thought you might die.

My great aunt, the one I called Grandma, treated me like her own child. She had only one son and two daughters: given the size of most families in Afghanistan it was like she was childless. She gave me a tiny aluminium case with a lock on it and made some clothing for me so that I could pack my case and go and sleep over at her place nearby. I felt so special and grown up. I loved it when she took me to visit her relatives, who were nomadic people and lived in a tent. They moved around the country depending on the season and when they were in Kabul she'd take me to see them. I remember every detail: the red Persian rug, the soft mattresses and pillows, the food that smelt and tasted so different to what my family ate.

Sometimes Grandma would even take me on holiday to Paghman, a few hours' drive from Kabul. It has since been wiped out by war, but back then cherries grew everywhere, there was a busy market, a park with a lake and a playground. It was really kind of her to take me because the car was crowded already with her own family. Sometimes there'd be fifteen of her relatives squashed into a sedan but she'd still find room to squeeze me in on her lap. There'd be kids in the boot even, but we all behaved – after all, even if we were being squashed, it was better than walking.

~

My brothers and sister and I slept in the same room, played together, talked together, loved and respected each other, but of course sometimes we'd fight. I think it was tough for my brother Assad because he was the third boy and didn't get as much attention after I was born. So he was always bothering me, taking my toys away from me and making me cry. One day when we were out playing in the yard he suggested we dig a hole in the ground and pretend to bake bread. So we dug a big hole and Assad set up a fire in the bottom. We made a loaf of bread out of mud, and he said to me, 'Your turn, you go and put the bread in the oven.' As I was putting the loaf in the hole he set alight a plastic bag and it landed on my hand, instantly melting onto my skin. I started screaming. My hand swelled up and I had to go and have it bandaged. Assad always said it was an accident.

Another time, I was playing with him on the second storey of our house and he hurt me somehow. Maybe he hit me, or maybe he just gave me a tiny little push – whichever it was, I called out for my mother, crying.

She came and scolded him: 'Why do you hurt Mahboba all the time?' She walked towards him, holding a stick as though she were about to hit him. 'You are never to touch this girl again,' she threatened.

He was standing by the window and said, 'Don't come near me, otherwise I'm going to throw myself out. You always blame me for everything.' She rushed over . . . and he jumped out the window.

I felt horrible. I thought my brother was dead because of me. My mother and I ran downstairs, screaming so loudly my aunts and cousins came running to see what had happened. Luckily there was a big tree next to the window and it had broken Assad's fall. He was badly hurt but he was alive. When he got up off the ground he said, 'You get away!' He was upset with me for a couple of weeks.

I loved my little sister Zarmina, but now I feel guilty when I think about how much work she used to do around the house compared to me. It wasn't like that to start with; I had always been good at housework. But when I was about seven I had my own mishap and everything changed.

Once a week my mother would take us all to the *hamam*, the public bath house. We would go there for two or three hours, until all the grime was steamed and scrubbed off us. One morning she took all the other kids to the *hamam* and asked me to do the housework and follow them there. I spent an hour or so cleaning the house from top to bottom, sweeping all the rooms and washing the dishes. My mother was very clean and taught us to be tidy all the time, so the house was sparkling when I locked the front door behind me.

My Uncle Khan Mohammed's house had a fruit tree out the front, a delicious Afghani fruit called *senjit*. As I walked past I noticed that there were a lot of *senjit* on that tree. It was a long walk to the steam room, about twenty minutes. I thought to myself, how about I take some of these fruit and eat them on the way? My auntie and uncle weren't home. I looked around to work out how to get my hands on the fruit. First I climbed up onto the roof of my auntie and uncle's toilet, and then scaled a mudbrick wall next to it. The problem was that the wall was extremely narrow, barely as wide as my foot; I had to balance on it like a cat. I walked slowly and carefully until I reached the tree. I grabbed a branch and started picking fruit and dropping them on the ground – I knew I'd lose my balance if I tried to put them in my pocket. My Uncle Haji's son, Freydoon, who was about four years old, appeared under the tree laughing, gobbling up the fruit as I dropped it, saying, 'Wow, what yummy *senjit*.'

I shouted down to him, 'I'm coming to get you. Do not touch my fruit!' As soon as I said it, my mind was no longer focused on balancing and I fell. I crashed onto the concrete below, face first. My head and face were bleeding. I started screaming as loud as I could. Freydoon ran and called his mother, my Aunt Rona. She found my older brother Omar and they took me to the hospital in a taxi. I lay on the ground in casualty for a few hours waiting for a doctor. Auntie Rona was crying because I was in so much pain. Omar begged the people behind the counter to do something but there were so many patients – many of them a lot worse than me – and very few doctors.

Normally we avoided disturbing my father at work but finally Omar called him, and then my father called the health minister. Suddenly I was on a trolley and they were preparing to take me to the operating room. Before I went under I saw my father and Omar talking with several doctors. It had been impossible to find even one doctor; now it seemed the whole hospital was here. It is amazing how much a little bit of power can achieve. One minute I was like a piece of rubbish, the next a queen. I had a bed, a painkilling injection and lots of nurses with white hats and white dresses rushing around me.

Both of my arms had been broken in three places: shoulders, elbows and wrists. I woke up with plaster casts on both arms and had to stay in hospital for a while. I remember my mother crying by my bedside. When I came home I found that my father had bought me a nice comfortable bed so I didn't have to sleep on the floor. There was a lovely bedspread, and on it a new doll. Grandma had brought it for me; she had come to stay for a couple of months to sleep by my side and help my mum look after me, because I couldn't do anything for myself. My bones had been broken in so many places that the doctors weren't sure whether I would ever be able to use my arms and hands fully again, and to help the bones knit I was supposed to rest. But that didn't stop me from giving my brothers and cousins a good whack with my casts if they annoyed me. It was summer – which in Kabul is stifling, with temperatures mostly in the mid to high thirties – and I was driven mad by my itchy skin under the plaster.

After a couple of months it was time to have the casts taken off, and my father went with me to the hospital. The doctor said that this was when we would know if the bones had healed properly and I would be able to use my hands. He cut the casts off. I felt nothing. My arms were numb and I couldn't lift them. I started crying, but the doctor said that my arms might just feel that way because I hadn't used them for so long. The real test was how the bones looked in an x-ray, so they took me to have one. They developed the film and the doctor said the bones had set well, but because I was so young and my bones were still growing, I was not to place stress on them. If I did, I might end up not being able to use my hands and arms at all. That meant no more lifting, no more carrying the shopping home, and no more housework. Even now as an adult, if I wash clothes by hand, lift heavy things or do a big job around the house like cleaning the windows, my wrists ache afterwards.

I quickly got used to not doing any work, and then I started to take it for granted that other people would do things for me. With eight children my mother couldn't handle all the housework herself. It was up to the girls in the family to help out, and that meant Zarmina. She became like another mother. By the time I woke up to go to school I usually saw clean laundry hanging out in the yard because Zarmina had got up at four o'clock in the morning and washed it all by hand. Doing the laundry was the most difficult, back-breaking job for a girl because you had to fill and carry big metal basins with hot water and sit on the ground, leaning over, scrubbing the clothes. Once they were dry she ironed them, and she helped my mother cook, bathed my younger brothers and did lots of other work around the house. Zarmina was too good. She never complained.

# Chapter 2

I started high school when I was about twelve. Everything to do with it was fun to me. I didn't want to miss a single day. I was friends with six or so girls in my class, all of us troublemakers. The teacher never saw us walk through the classroom door because we always jumped in through the windows. And when the bell rang at the end of the class we jumped out again. If we had a test that day we might get the whole class to refuse to do it, so the teacher would have to reschedule it for another day.

We laughed all the time, sometimes at nothing, but we were smart and studied a lot, too. Many of the girls at my school didn't consider education important because they knew they would only be there until they were about fourteen, the usual time for girls to get married. My friends and I wanted to stay at school so that we could go to university and become doctors. It was an exciting time for young women in Afghanistan. The government had finally made it possible for women to get an education and have a career if we wanted. It all came down to the attitude of your family. My father wanted me to be educated and able to look after myself – and I was lucky enough to be living in a time when the community and the government couldn't stop me.

My friends and I knew that we would have to have excellent results to get into medicine so we worked hard, right from the start of high school. On the weekends we'd go to each other's houses to study. Whatever questions the teachers asked us in class we always knew the answers, so they couldn't really punish us for misbehaving.

At lunchtime we'd get together with about six other friends from another class and cause havoc. We always got served quickly at the cafeteria because they were so keen to get us out of there. Our favourite pastime was tricking the school guard, who kept the keys for all the rooms in the school on a key ring in his shirt pocket. He was old and forever falling asleep on his chair at the front entrance. We'd tie a magnet to a length of cotton thread and lower it into his pocket, then slowly pull the magnet out with the keys stuck to it. Sometimes he'd wake up. We'd run off and he'd come charging after us, trying to get close enough to smack us.

Some days he wouldn't wake up at all and we would go and unlock the assembly hall, which was only used a few times a year for special events. It had a stage and hundreds of padded chairs for the audience to sit on. We'd get up on stage and put on our own plays, sing songs, recite poems, dance, or just shout and run around. We all had a lot of energy to burn off because there were no sports for girls to play. All we had was a basketball team, but there were only fifteen places in the team and about three thousand girls in our school.

When we had finished performing we'd go and give the keys back to the guard. We'd kiss his hand and give him food and beg him not to tell the teachers we'd stolen his keys. And most of the time he didn't. We made his life difficult but really we loved the old man.

During school holidays I missed seeing my friends every day. School closed down for three months each winter because it snowed heavily in Kabul. The weeks dragged by as I sat with my cousins and aunties looking out through the windows as everything turned white. In summer the city sweated and we had three or four weeks off. My mother would take my brothers, Zarmina and me to my grandmother's place in Panjshir Valley. Up there in the mountains amongst her grapevines it was much cooler.

One year we went off on our summer holiday a month early. My mother was seven months pregnant and had bad morning sickness. What she needed was to go and rest and be with my grandmother. My father stayed in Shahr-e-now with my two oldest brothers, Omar and Anwar.

We'd been with my grandmother for three weeks when Omar, Anwar and two of my older male cousins arrived unexpectedly. They had come to tell my mother that while we'd been in Abdara my father had married a second wife. I will never forget the sound of my mother crying, screaming and shouting after they told her. She had suspected for a while that my father was looking for a second wife. She always got nervous when he was around women or travelled overseas for work.

In Afghanistan it was rare to meet someone, fall in love and then marry. You had a marriage arranged for you, usually by a family member. One of my father's relatives had told him about a nice girl named Nadira, who was from Kabul and about the same age as my eldest brother, Anwar. My father had proposed and her parents, knowing that he was quite well off and could look after their daughter, had accepted.

People were used to men taking extra wives because it had been part of our tradition for thousands of years, but that didn't mean everyone was happy about it. It wasn't always well accepted by the community, unless the man's first wife hadn't been able to bear children or wasn't fulfilling her duties as a wife in some other way – and neither of these were the case with my mother. A few of my father's relatives didn't go to the wedding, instead staying home with Anwar and Omar.

A first wife was usually devastated but had no choice – she had to accept the situation. In Afghanistan it was nearly impossible for a woman to survive without a husband because there were few opportunities for her to earn a living and no financial support from the government. For a woman with children it was even harder: if a divorced woman remarried, her first husband could automatically take custody of the children they'd had together, and she might never see them again.

We set off for Kabul straight after we heard the news, though my grandmother begged my mother to stay with her and send us back to Kabul to live with him. She walked by my mother's side as we went along the narrow mountain path to catch the bus, pleading with her: 'Don't go, don't go. Stay here, let the kids go. Stay here and when the baby comes, send it to him.'

My mother cried: 'I can't leave my children.' We knew that our mother would never leave us but we felt scared and uncertain about the future anyway.

When we arrived home my mother discovered that my father's wardrobe was empty. He had moved into Nadira's parents' house. My mother could not cope. She paced during the night; she paced during the day. Some nights we found her up on the roof. Maybe she was looking up at the stars praying to God for advice.

After we'd been home a week my father returned. If a husband takes more than one wife he must spend equal time with them and treat them the same. He has to spend one night with one wife and the next with the other. If he buys something for one, he has to buy the same for the other. But when my father returned to spend time with my mother she grabbed hold of him and started shaking him. I watched from the corner of the room as she hit him and shouted and screamed and bit the finger he was wearing his new wedding ring on. He had never worn a wedding ring before. My father just stood there; he didn't defend himself.

Eventually my mother calmed down enough for them to talk. He told her he'd buy her anything she wanted or do anything to please her. He promised he would come and spend every second night with her. He would do everything he could for us children. He would still be the man of the house. 'This is what God chose for me. I love my kids and I will look after you.'

She said: 'I no longer accept you. From this moment, I don't know you as my husband. I will stay with my children; I am the mother of my children, but I will have nothing to do with you.' My mother's voice was quiet but hard like steel. My father was stunned and silent. I admired my mother. It was incredibly brave of her at that time, in that environment, to say to her husband: 'No, I don't want you.' She kept her word – she wouldn't have allowed him to so much as hold her hand again.

My father started living permanently with his new wife. For a few months, because Yama was only two years old or so and cried for his father, he came to visit us every few weeks. We older children didn't make him feel as welcome, though, and he began to visit less and less often.

My mother was probably only in her early thirties and a beautiful woman, but my father was the first man in her life and my father was the last one. She did cry. She did love him. We heard her say many times that our father had not been a bad husband, that he had treated her well and that when he had gone overseas for work she had missed him.

My mother gave birth to her ninth child, a girl whom she named Zargona. There was no money coming into the household now my father was living with Nadira, and no such thing as a single mother's benefit. Omar solved the problem by finding us a house to rent in a cheaper area of Kabul, called Khair Khana. We rented out our place in Shahr-e-now and paid for food and other expenses with the money that was left after we'd paid the rent on our new place. The houses in Khair Khana were smaller and more rundown than those in Shahr-e-now. We had gone from a three-storey house with a modern kitchen to a one-storey with with the kitchen outside. Inside, there was a storage room piled high with clothes and mattresses, a bedroom and a visitors room. Hospitality is so important in Afghanistan that no matter how bad things get, you always have a visitors room. Normally it was kept locked because it had to be spotless in case a guest arrived unexpectedly, but now that Anwar and Omar had grown up they slept there. My mother, my six other brothers and sisters and I crammed into the bedroom, which was only just big enough for us to lie down in.

The house was full of cockroaches. We kept the house spotless and sprayed insecticide but it only kept them away for two or three weeks at a time because they were constantly hatching in the earth under our floor. As we slept the cockroaches walked all over us and sometimes crawled into our mouths.

Moving to Khair Khana was like dropping out of the sky and crashing to the ground. And the worst thing wasn't the cockroaches or the tiny house – it was leaving behind our cousins. Even though they came to visit us it wasn't the same as having them around all the time.

Soon after my parents split up Anwar moved to Iran because he could earn more money there. Many people in Afghanistan, including my family, speak Dari, which is closely related to the language spoken in Iran, Farsi. The two countries also share similar cultures, so many Afghanis go to live there. Anwar started working in a shoe store in the capital, Tehran, and was soon earning enough money to send some back home to us each month.

My second-eldest brother, Omar, who was only in year ten at school, now took on the role of man of the house, just as my father had done for his brothers and sisters. Omar was an open-minded, smart, understanding boy with a gift for writing poetry. From the moment he became the head of the household he had a very positive impact on my life. He carried on raising us to be the kind of people my father wanted us to be – honest, well behaved and well educated – but he brought a new feeling of openness and freedom to our house. Whatever we were having trouble with at school he'd teach us at night, spending hours with us like a tutor. He was only a teenager but had to be a brother and a father and look after my mother as well. He was wonderful with Zargona and for many years she thought that he was her father.

My mother suddenly had a lot more freedom than when we lived with my father. In Shahr-e-now she hardly ever went out except when she needed to buy something special, like a dress to wear to a wedding, but now she went out every day to do the shopping. Financially things were okay, thanks to Anwar sending money over and Omar organising our household and the renting of our house in Shahr-e-now. Gradually the smile returned to her face.

~

After we moved to Khair Khana I kept going to school in Shahr-e-now; my brothers and Zarmina all went to school in Khair Khana. It took me an hour and a half to get to school because I had to take two buses and walk a long way, but it was a good school, I loved my friends, and I enjoyed travelling across the city.

I wanted to start wearing make-up but my mother and Omar wouldn't allow me to because they didn't want me attracting boys. When I was with my friends we'd dip a nail into cheap black shoe polish and apply it like mascara to our eyelashes. It was okay so long as it didn't rain or you didn't cry. We'd take a fresh walnut hanging from a tree, pull the hull off it and rub it on our lips. It would stain our lips bright red for a couple of weeks. And when we put Vaseline over the top it really looked like lipstick. If my mother or Omar asked about it I'd say innocently that I'd just been eating walnuts.

The reason they didn't want me attracting boys was that reputation was everything. If a girl was known to have gone out with a boy in the past, the family of any would-be husband would probably refuse her. That's if she could find a would-be husband: boys would often go out with girls, but only marry the kind of girl who didn't go out with boys. And it wasn't just the girl's reputation that would be damaged. Her family's would also be wrecked, especially that of her father and brothers. In traditional Afghani society a girl's virtue belonged to the male members of her family, and if she lost her virtue it reflected badly on them, too. Even though Kabul had become a slightly more modern city in the last few years, with girls and women allowed to choose whether to completely cover themselves with a *burqa*, just wear a scarf on their heads or not cover themselves at all, traditional attitudes to how women should behave with men were still strong.

Boys from a school nearby would hang around outside our school every afternoon when the bell rang. If a boy saw a girl he liked he'd follow her onto her bus, get off at her stop and follow her all the way home. He'd do this a few days in a row. Should the girl give him a signal, such as smiling at him, he might slip a love letter inside a book and give it to her, then ask her out. Most girls ignored boys but a handful ran the risk and went out with them, maybe to the cinema or for a walk somewhere. By Australian standards it was innocent, but it could spell the end of a girl's future and shame for her family. It could even end in bloodshed for the boy's or the girl's family.

I never went out with boys no matter how much they pestered me. I didn't give a damn about boys. I acted like a boy myself. I admit that I liked it when they followed me home and tried to slip me love letters because it made me feel attractive, but I was only interested in having them as friends. And even if I'd wanted to I wouldn't have gone out with a boy because I didn't want Omar to suffer the shame and embarrassment.

That's not to say I didn't disobey Omar. I often did things he'd forbidden me from doing – but only for innocent fun. When I was about thirteen, a big celebration was planned to mark an important national holiday in Afghanistan. There was to be an event at a stadium in Kabul, attended by the president. It was to open with hundreds of Kabul school students performing a choreographed routine, just as they do at big sporting events like the Olympics. Omar said I couldn't be involved because it would mean mixing with boys at the practice sessions every day.

Each morning I woke up at five o'clock to put on my costume – modern-looking, tight white pants and tight, bright orange top – and my boot polish and Vaseline make-up. It was summertime and in summer Omar always laid his mattress in the garden, just outside the front door, and slept there like a guard. In the dark I would slowly open the door, hoping that it wouldn't creak, and creep past Omar on tiptoe to go and catch the bus to the stadium for rehearsals. I did this for a couple of months.

Even though Omar, as the man of the house, had the final say I had asked my mother's permission and she had said, 'Okay, but be careful that he doesn't catch you.' I told Zarmina too, and took her along with me a couple of times, which she loved. My mother and Zarmina and I were always on each other's side. Omar only found out about it after the performance, and by then all he could do was laugh.

# Chapter 3

I liked sleeping in the same room with my mum and brothers and sisters. It was comforting to hear their breathing and know they were near me. So why was my heart thudding? Something had woken me up in the middle of the night. A buzzing sound. I was confused, half asleep, trying to work out what it was. It got louder and louder until *shoooo*, it passed over the house, rattling the windows. There was a deep rumbling, like thunder, after it had gone.

Zargona started crying. I heard my mother trying to soothe her. We were all awake now, but too scared to get up and turn the light on. The buzzing built up again, until *shoooo*, another plane – I realised that was the only thing it could be – roared low overhead. One after the other they flew over. I hid under my blankets hoping they would stop, but they just kept coming.

As soon as the sun came up we got out of bed and put the radio on. What the announcer said made no sense to me: the Russian army had occupied Kabul. We rushed into our front yard. The city I'd known had been replaced by something from a nightmare. There were tanks rolling down the street and the sky was full of warplanes.

~

What did the Russians want from us? Like most women and girls in Afghanistan I had no idea about politics and current affairs. I knew our country's history was filled with conflict. At school I'd learned that one after the other we'd fought off the invading armies of the Greeks, Alexander the Great, Genghis Khan, Tamerlane, the Moghuls. Afghanistan was important to them because we were at the crossroads of trade routes between southern and eastern Asia, the Middle East and Europe. The British had tried to make us part of their empire but we forced them out in the early 1900s. What none of the invaders realised was how harsh the mountains and deserts of Afghanistan were, and how much Afghanis love their country and independence, and are prepared to fight for them.

I had thought this was all just something you studied in history, but suddenly there was an invading army right in the middle of our capital city. The cycle was repeating itself.

I now learned that the year before, 1978, while I had

been having food fights in the cafeteria, our prime minister had been assassinated and his government overthrown by communists. The new communist government had brought in reforms that involved taking farming land from some people and redistributing it to others. The reforms went against thousands of years of Afghani tradition, and land-owners in the countryside got angry about it and put up an armed struggle against the government officials who were trying to implement the policy. The army had to step in, but the fighting spread into rural towns. Soldiers who were unhappy about fighting their own people for the sake of communist reforms they didn't even believe in deserted or mutinied and the army started to fall apart. The government called on the Russians for help. It would be embarrassing for the Russians for a communist regime to fail so they started to send soldiers and weapons to help put down the revolts in the countryside.

The revolts got worse, though, and finally the Russians, unhappy with the way the president was handling things, invaded. What had woken us that night was the sound of hundreds of Soviet army transport planes coming in to land at the airport. While they were rumbling overhead the Russians had taken the palace and killed the president so that they could install someone who would do what he was told.

After the invasion, life was put on hold. We were all in a state of shock. Hardly anyone went out on the street, partic-ularly women and girls. We stayed inside our homes. It was winter so there was no school, but we even stopped going out to shop or visit people. I sat inside with my school books but it was hard to concentrate knowing that outside there were soldiers everywhere.

When the school year of 1980 started many parents were too scared to let their daughters leave their houses. Announcements came over the radio advising people that school was back to normal and encouraging us to return. Many girls never did. I returned to school, but there didn't seem much point because communist doctrine had become more important than maths or science. Our principal sided with the communist regime, as did a handful of the teachers. Often we'd have to go to the assembly hall to hear the pro-communist teachers read out Marxist–Leninist writings. They called Russia the brother country and said they were coming to help us. A few times they picked out the nicest-looking girls, taught them communist songs, gave them bright costumes and made them perform on TV. They chose a close friend of mine. She didn't believe the words of the communist songs but she performed them anyway because she was scared that otherwise her family might be put in jail.

Anybody who raised their voice against Russia was put in jail or executed. At the prison at Pul-i-charki, a suburb on the outskirts of Kabul, political prisoners were tortured and killed every day. It is believed that the regime dug big pits to bury executed prisoners in, using bulldozers to cover them with soil. Some say that not all the prisoners were dead before they were buried and that the ground would keep moving for three or four days afterwards. I'd had hardly any experience of death before, but now I heard of people being killed all the time – school friends' brothers, sisters, cousins, mothers, fathers . . .

It was amazing how fast things started to fall apart. Farming was disrupted and the economy ground to a halt. We hadn't been a rich country before, but nearly everyone had had enough to eat. Now food was scarce and there were people begging on the streets.

Within a few months the shock of being invaded had worn off, and then we got angry. Nearly everyone in Afghanistan is Muslim. We didn't want to be governed by communists who believed there should be no religion at all. And we love our independence so we certainly didn't want to be governed by Russians: our president might have been Afghani but it was obvious he'd been put there by the Russians.

There is something in Afghani people's blood that when someone invades us we fight. People were fleeing to nearby Pakistan and from there the men started to form groups of freedom fighters, called Mujaheddin. They regularly mounted attacks on the Russian troops in the countryside. In the city, workers went on strike and held huge demonstrations, and hundreds of them were killed by Russian troops.

One day at school word went around that the boys from the school near us were planning their own demonstration. All the girls wanted to join them. The excitement started to build when some of the older girls sent around a whispered message that we should be prepared to march some time the following day. Shortly after we'd gone into class the next morning, the bell rang. The teachers had to let us stream out of our classrooms into the playground in case it was a fire alarm. But there was no fire. A girl in year twelve, Shakila, was at the front gate ringing the bell. She shouted out to gather together and get ready to march out of the school into the streets. Shakila was a beautiful girl – fair-skinned, blonde and green-eyed – as well as strong and brave. Looking at her up the front, not scared of the principal or soldiers, made the rest of us feel brave, too.

The gate was locked so as a group we all surged forward and pushed until the lock broke. We spilled out onto the road and started marching toward the boys school. All three thousand girls from our school joined the march. The girls at the front would start a chant and it would spread through the crowd until we were all screaming: 'Russia, out, out, out!' or 'Death to Russia!'. We had tears running down our faces.

When we got to the boys school we shouted as loud as we could until the boys came out to follow behind us. Still chanting, we headed to Kabul University, which was about a two-hour walk. We joined thousands of university and high school students there. Reaching the uni grounds and seeing the thousands of young people screaming and chanting, all of them as angry and passionate as me, was a turning point in my life. I knew then that I had to devote myself to getting Russia out of our country. I wasn't interested in education any more. My dreams had been destroyed. I had no future. I wanted Russia out – or death.

Our school started protesting three or four times a week. We would march through the school gate and go to the university, collecting students from other schools along the way. Occasionally university students gave speeches in front of the crowd, but they always ended up in jail the next day. Students came to the demonstrations from schools all over Kabul. The massive peace rallies in Australia in 2003 against the war in Iraq reminded me of our protests. Each one took a whole day, and when we weren't protesting we were planning the next one.

I joined a group of about twenty-five other girls to help out with the planning and preparations for the protests. We organised girls to make flags and paint banners with slogans like 'Russia out', and got hold of a loudspeaker so that everyone could hear the chant and follow along. The traffic stopped for us. Men and women who lived in the houses along the path of our marches shouted out their support. The guard whose keys we used to steal now handed them over willingly so that we could open the school gate. 'I am proud of you,' he'd say. After a while the principal realised the old man was helping us and suddenly we had a new guard. We always managed to break through the gate though. Most of the teachers were on our side and didn't make it difficult for us to go and protest. As soon as Shakila rang the bell they opened the doors and let us go.

The soldiers were always trying to stop us from protesting. Some days their tanks would block our path completely and we'd have no choice but to go back to school. The Russian soldiers had fair skin, rosy red cheeks, green eyes and blond hair. I knew that they were extremely handsome men, but no matter how handsome they were they looked ugly to me.

At other times soldiers would come on foot to break up our demonstrations, moving through the crowd and hitting girls with batons. I got hit so many times I lost count. They stopped just short of shooting us. Once when we were throwing rocks at a group of Russian soldiers driving past in a jeep I hit one near his temple and he started to bleed. He was furious and raised his rifle and aimed it right at me. At the last minute he managed to control himself and lowered his weapon, but one of the Afghani soldiers who had been sent to control our demonstration chased after me and hit me so hard with a baton that I had a black bruise covering one whole buttock for three months.

The Afghani army had shrunk since the Russian invasion because many Afghani soldiers had deserted and joined the resistance. There was a conscription program but most young men fled the country before they were old enough to be conscripted. What was left of the army fought alongside the Russians, under their control. One day when we were demonstrating I saw a boy who had lived in my street in Shahr-e-now. We used to take our clothes to be repaired by his father, the local tailor. Nageeb, who was about eighteen, was wearing the Afghani army uniform. He had a baton and was walking through the crowd, hitting my schoolmates. He was about to hit me when he recognised me and lowered his baton. I took off my scarf, put it on his head, tied it up for him and said, 'You are a woman. Don't call yourself a man because you are not a man. We are the men.' All the girls started laughing at him. 'How could you hit your own citizens, your own sisters?' I said. He looked ridiculous trying to get the scarf off without letting go of his gun or his stick. I was lucky that he was too ashamed to retaliate.

Often the soldiers would round up two or three hundred girls at the front of the protest and take us into detention. There were so many of us that they had to occupy unused government offices because there was nowhere else to hold us. They would write down our names and search through our bags, looking for anything that could link us to the resistance against the government. Girls who were found with Mujaheddin membership cards in their bags were taken to prison. The rest of us were let go at the end of the day with a warning that we mightn't be so lucky next time. Their idea was to scare us but it wouldn't have mattered what they'd done. Nothing would have stopped us.

The regime's other weapon was the secret police, or Khad. The Khad had spies everywhere. It was a time of paranoia. Neighbours, friends and sometimes even family members were too scared to say what they really felt about the Russians to each other in case it got reported to the Khad or someone who worked in the government. My own family was to learn just how powerful, and devastating, informers could be.

My twenty-three-year-old cousin Sarwar, who was the son of one of my mother's sisters, was in love with a woman named Zargona and wanted to marry her. She was an educated, modern woman who worked as an accountant. She loved Sarwar and wanted to marry him but her family had arranged for her to wed somebody else. One day she secretly fled her home and took shelter at my aunt's house. My aunt and uncle did not feel they could turn her away and despite the possible consequences they organised a proper Islamic wedding for the couple. Even though we were living in a time of great upheaval, tradition was still important in Afghanistan. Zargona had shamed her family and ruined their reputation. Her brothers and father were terribly angry with her and with Sarwar.

I would often go and visit Sarwar and Zargona in the afternoon. It was beautiful to see how much they loved each other. They didn't have a traditional Afghani relationship. Sarwar treated Zargona like a queen. He often did the housework and when she came home from work he'd have a cup of tea ready for her.

After they'd been together for three months they went to make peace with Zargona's family but were rejected. One morning three months after that, Sarwar went to his job at Kabul airport and never returned. We looked for Sarwar for almost a year, then one night we heard news that Pul-i-charki prison was about to post a list of people who had died there. The next day my aunt, my mother and I went to look at the list and saw his name there. My aunt and my mum fell to their knees, sobbing.

Zargona's family worked in the government. All they had to do was tell the Khad that Sarwar was a Mujaheddin.

That was their revenge, their way of restoring their family's honour. His body was never returned and no grave was ever found. Kind, loving and funny Sarwar was probably buried in a mass grave.

Most men Sarwar's age passed illegally over the border into Pakistan or Iran, at the risk of being caught and imprisoned or shot by the regime rather than lose their freedom. My brother Assad was conscripted but instead fled to Tehran, where he helped Anwar in the shoe shop. Omar went to stay with friends in a village for his safety. It was especially upsetting when Omar left because it was like we were losing another father. My mother kept a pair of his shoes by the door, as if he were still with us.

I became the man of the house. I helped my younger brothers and sisters with their homework and went to speak to their teachers about how they were going at school, as Omar had done. It was hard for my brothers to send money back to us in Kabul without the money going missing or the Khad finding out that we had family who had fled the regime. Anwar sent money to us through people who were travelling from Tehran to Kabul, or he transferred money to us through a business in a rough district of Kabul where women rarely went. Every now and then I would have to go there and collect the cash and walk home with it. It was dangerous for me to carry money on my own in that area but because of the way I walked, talked and dealt with men, they didn't trouble me. They treated me like a man. I remembered how my father had taught me to walk home with the shopping though it was usually considered a man's or a boy's job. I don't think even he could have foreseen how much our lives would change and how useful his training would be.

~

One morning Shakila didn't come to school. We waited for her to ring the bell to start a protest but the bell only rang at the usual break times and at the end of school. The next day she still wasn't at school, and her parents sent no word about her. No-one wanted to say what we all knew deep down: we would never see Shakila again. Either she'd had to flee the country or was in Pul-i-charki, or maybe she had been murdered already.

My friends and I were upset, sad and angry all at once. The one thing we were not was scared. No doubt the government had hoped that Shakila's disappearance would frighten us so much we'd call off our protests. But it only made us more determined to get the Russians out of our country. We couldn't let Shakila's life be ruined or end so young for nothing. The rest of us owed it to her to keep fighting.

We had never voted for an official leader of our protests. Shakila had just naturally stepped into the role, along with a few other girls. Now that she was gone we didn't have any formal discussions about who would take her place, we just kept on getting together for meetings, painting banners, thinking up new chants or demonstration routes. But gradually I noticed that when a decision needed to be made about something the rest of the girls were turning to me.

More and more often it was me ringing the bell. I found myself standing in front of the whole school with the loud-hailer giving instructions, and the girls followed them. I was becoming one of the protest leaders. I was becoming somebody I never realised I could be.

One of my father's brothers, Uncle Khan Mohammed, heard from someone at his work that I was leading anti-government protests and that if I wasn't careful I'd soon be heading to jail. He passed this on to my father. I was at a demonstration when I saw him riding his bicycle not far from the marchers, watching me. At the end of the rally he rode up and asked me to stop protesting – or at least to stay at the back of the crowd where the soldiers and Khad couldn't see me. He knew how the regime worked. He said that if I was sent to jail there was a high chance I would be killed, but if I wasn't my life would be ruined anyway. Girls who went to prison were raped repeatedly by soldiers – and in Afghanistan once a girl lost her virginity no-one would marry her, even though it obviously wasn't her fault. I believed that what he was saying was true and that he was giving me this warning out of love but I didn't care, I was going to keep on protesting anyway.

My mother, on the other hand, never asked me to stop. She wanted me to fight for my country. She worried about me all the time and would have been devastated if anything had happened to me, but she was willing to make that sacri-fice. She was a brave mother. My father was opposed to the communist regime but if he had protested he would've lost his job and been unable to support his family.

Omar risked his life every couple of months to come and see how we were doing. One time Anwar came from Tehran instead. When he saw how much the situation in Kabul had deteriorated Anwar became concerned about us living alone with no man to protect us. In Afghani culture it is almost unheard of for women to live without adult male relatives, and with the chaos in Kabul it now seemed unsafe. He was worried about what the Russian soldiers might do to my mother, Zarmina and me. His fears were understandable. So many girls and women had been taken by Russian soldiers near the *hamam* that we'd stopped going there.

One day I said to myself, 'Why should I let the Russians ruin my life?' and off I went. I soaked myself for an hour or two and left feeling great: I had a colourful towel wrapped around my hair, my face was shiny and clean, I'd just changed into fresh clothes. Then I saw a truck full of Russian soldiers. One of the soldiers looked straight into my eyes. I immediately looked down at the ground. I started to shake because of what I'd seen in his eyes: he had looked at me the way a lion looks at its prey. I walked towards a fruit shop a few doors down. The soldier said something to me in Russian, then something to the others, and I heard the truck reverse towards me. I dropped my dirty clothes and ran into the shop and hid behind the man who owned it. A few people gathered around and finally the soldiers drove off. I didn't go to the *hamam* again after that.

Anwar discussed our situation with my father. Soon after that my father came to see my mother and told her he was worried about us and he'd like us all to go and live with him. It was clear to her that with six children, including two teenage girls, it was the safest thing to do. We packed up and moved in with my father, his wife Nadira, and their three children in Khair Khana. They had one small room to spare for us. We ate there, slept there, studied there, and it was our visitors room too. It was hardest for my mother. Before, she'd made the decisions about what the family would eat each day, and she'd gone out and done the shopping. At my father's place he did those things.

Nadira was only ten years or so older than me so we had a similar outlook and got on well, but it upset my mother to hear my father and her talking affectionately to each other. Every evening they would go out in the garden to water the chillies and tomatoes and they'd talk to each other like a couple in love. Their every action and word hurt her. Even when my father gave my mother a little money to spend she wasn't interested in buying anything for herself. Three of her boys were gone, the country was in a terrible state, she'd lost her house, and now she had to watch my father with his new wife. Her way of coping with the situation was to spend as much time away as she could. She went and stayed with one of my aunties, who lived down the road, or at my grandmother's place in Panjshir Valley. She always took Zargona with her, and Zarmina and I looked after our brothers.

One time when my mother was on the way to my grandmother's place we heard on the radio that there was heavy fighting in Panjshir Valley. The valley was so steep and remote that it made the perfect hiding place for

Mujaheddin, and the Russians had sent in ground forces and planes to try to wipe them out. They didn't just target the Mujaheddin though, they bombed and burnt down villages and left many ordinary people dead. I couldn't stop thinking about little Zargona. The last time I saw her she was so full of life. After three weeks without hearing from my mother I went to the house of one of my aunties and she asked a relative who was also from Abdara to go and see if my mother and Zargona were still alive. The road was blocked by the Russians and he couldn't get through. No-one could get in or out of Panjshir Valley, and no news could get in or out either.

It was two months before my mother could send word to us that she and Zargona were okay. When the fighting had started they'd hidden in a cornfield. The people who lived in the village they were passing through had shouted at them to get down on their stomachs and stay completely still. Zargona was only three and it was the first time she'd been in a cornfield. She got excited and jumped up to shake one of the cornstalks. The Russians saw the movement and started shooting. A few villagers lost their lives.

Once the shooting had stopped my mother ran and hid with Zargona under a nearby bridge. A soldier took pity on them. Afghanistan is made up of several ethnic groups, such as Pashtun, Tajik, Uzbek and Hazara, who speak a number of languages. This soldier was Tajik, the same ethnic group as us, so he understood the language my mother was speaking, Dari. Tajik people are also found in the neighbouring country of Tajikistan, which was under Russian control. The Russians had brought in many soldiers from Tajikistan because they thought they would not only be able to fight the Mujaheddin but also help win the support of Afghani Tajiks. But the soldiers from Tajikistan identified with other Tajiks and ended up helping us rather than trying to turn us into good communists. The soldier led my mother and Zargona to safety in another village, walking with them and hiding them from the Russian soldiers.

I hugged my mother and Zargona so hard when they finally came home about three months after they had left. I spoke to my mother about Nadira and asked her to try and accept her, rather than risking her own and Zargona's life by going to Panjshir Valley all the time. My mother realised that Nadira had done nothing wrong. She started to build a good relationship with her and began to spend more time at home.

# Chapter 4

As the occupation dragged into its third year Russia was bogged down all over the country trying to fight the Mujaheddin. Thousands of their soldiers – and far more Afghanis – had been killed but we weren't showing any signs of giving up. The protests in Kabul got bigger and more vocal, and the soldiers became more desperate to get us under control.

By now we'd become a lot more organised and a lot more creative with our protests. A group of about twenty-five of us would meet every morning in the toilets down the bottom of the schoolyard, where we wouldn't be seen by the principal. For a long time we'd talked about how much we hated that our school library was filled with books about Marx, Lenin and Stalin that had been translated into Dari. We believed that these books were the Russians' way of brainwashing us. At a meeting, a girl suggested that we should burn these books and everyone thought it was a great idea. We had a few meetings to work out how we would do it.

First our group of twenty-five girls went to the library and pulled every communist book we could find off the shelves. There was no time to carefully read the title of each book but they always had Marx, Lenin or Stalin on the cover so someone shouted out to grab 'the books with beards and moustaches on the covers'. We threw the books in heaps on the floor. Then we ran from classroom to classroom telling the other girls to help us take them out into the playground, right in front of the school – and the principal's window. Girls charged in and grabbed armfuls of books and ran out to the playground and threw them in a pile. It built up quickly and soon all the communist books were stacked up like a small mountain.

We set it alight. Gradually the fire took hold and the whole lot went up. There was so much smoke that people came running from all over Shahr-e-now to see if the school was on fire. Six of us started dancing in a ring around the fire. We clapped and sang out anti-Russian slogans. A teacher came over and said, 'Why are you dancing around the fire? The principal will know you organised this.' We were so young and caught up in the moment we didn't think about the future; we kept dancing. The principal came out of his office and watched us for a while, then wrote down our names on a notepad. I don't remember receiving any punishment at the time, but now that I had brought myself to the principal's attention I was worried about what might happen to me in the future.

Later that year the regime took a new approach to trying to turn us into good communists: bribery. A truck pulled up at the school gate and men started unloading boxes and taking them to the assembly hall. Inside the boxes there were colourful new dresses, headscarves and earrings handmade across the border in Uzbekistan. And there were new shoes of a kind we'd never seen before: trainers. The principal made an announcement. At the end of the day we were to go to the assembly hall and take something for ourselves and each member of our family. Lots of people in Kabul could barely afford to eat let alone buy clothes, and now they were giving us them for free.

The group of girls who organised the protests immediately went down to the toilets in the schoolyard to have a meeting about what we should do. At first we decided that we should tell all the girls in the school to simply not go into the assembly hall to collect the clothes. Then it occurred to us that our protest would have more impact if the girls collected all the clothes but then set fire to them.

We sent word around to all the classes in the school and when the bell rang at the end of the day the girls quietly and politely lined up in the assembly hall and took armfuls of clothes. The girls were so well behaved the principal had no idea we were planning something. Normally we would've loved to have worn new dresses, shoes and jewellery but I don't remember one single girl taking anything home. The clothes were from the government so they may as well have been dirt to us.

We left the school grounds and started to build a pile in a nearby street where there were lots of shops and people passing by. Someone lit it and girls added their clothes to the fire one by one. With three thousand girls in the school it took ages and the fire became very high. This time we were smart enough not to be seen around the fire; as soon as a girl had thrown her clothes into the flames she went home or, like me and my friends, stood at a distance watching.

The smoke smelt horrible because of the burning rubber in the soles of the running shoes. The fire started to burn almost out of control, nearly setting alight the nearby shops, and the principal had to call the fire brigade. The shop owners hated the regime too and didn't make trouble for us, even though we'd put their shops in danger.

~

Every high school in Kabul held demonstrations and I got to know the organisers from other schools. I became good friends with a girl named Gita from another school; she was a tall, strong girl and was very active in the protest movement. Her father had died in Pul-i-charki for being anti-government and her mother, to ensure the safety of her children, had made friends with members of the Khad. Gita had to keep her protesting secret from her. I went to Gita's house once and we could only whisper about protesting after we had gone into another room and closed the door and curtains.

One morning the Khad went to Gita's home and took her to be interrogated. Her mother went along with her. They were taken to see one of Gita's mother's friends. He said to Gita's mother: 'Your daughter has gone too far now, but I'm going to do you both a favour.' He said he'd make sure she wasn't sent to Pul-i-charki so long as she told him which protest group she was involved in and the names of the girls she protested with. Gita refused to betray any of her friends but her mother was desperate to protect her and said: 'Mahboba'. Then she gave him my address.

As soon as they let Gita go she ran straight to my place and told my mother, 'Tonight your house is going to be searched. Don't let Mahboba come home. They will put her in prison.'

What they didn't know was that I was already on my way there.

~

The day had begun like many school days: I rang the bell shortly after class had started so that the girls would assemble for a demonstration. We were met in the school ground by rows of soldiers aiming their guns at us. The school was surrounded by tanks. A soldier yelled at us through a loudspeaker to go back to our classrooms and that if we didn't do as he said we would be shot. Soldiers fired warning shots into the sky. We ran back into the school. The soldiers let off tear gas. The gas ate into my eyes; I felt like I was going blind. No-one said a word or screamed; we just ran. Somehow I managed to find my classroom.

Five soldiers and a few other people who I guessed were from the government or Khad came in behind us. The soldiers aimed their guns at the class. The government people stood silently scanning the room for a long time then started pointing at certain girls, telling them to get up and go out into the hallway. Out of the classroom window I could see buses pulling up in the schoolyard. They weren't our normal school buses. I knew I was finished.

I remembered my father saying that in jail I'd be raped every night. I kept thinking of a story I'd heard about a group of village girls on their way to a wedding. There were nine of them, dressed in their prettiest clothes. Some Russian soldiers saw the girls, grabbed them and put them into a helicopter. The villagers saw the helicopter take off and then the girls' colourful dresses falling down out of the blue sky. They never saw the girls again. I looked at the window and thought I would rather die here at school than be raped by soldiers. If I ran to jump out I would be shot and it would all be over. One of my friends was sitting next to me. Years ago we'd jumped in and out of the classroom window together to annoy our teachers. She saw me staring at the window and took hold of my hand. She held it down really hard on the desk. It was her silent way of saying, 'No jumping today.'

I stayed in my seat until a man out the front pointed at

me, then I got up and shakily walked to the door. I waited
with the other girls in the corridor until there were about
ten or fifteen of us and the soldiers escorted us out into the
schoolyard. The same thing was going on in all the other
classrooms. I was told to wait with a group of two hundred
or so girls. Some of the girls were really brave. Some cried.
Some collapsed. I felt numb. There were four or five buses
parked inside the school grounds.

Mothers and fathers of students were lining the footpaths
outside the school gates desperately trying to see the faces of
their children but I didn't see any of my family out there.
After about three hours a soldier told the group of girls I was
with to file onto the buses. They packed as many of us into
each bus as they possibly could, and we drove through the
school gates. There were no soldiers on the bus but in front
and behind us was a jeep carrying two soldiers. As soon as
we left the school grounds, girls started shouting out the
windows to people on the street. They yelled out things like:
'We are dying for our country!' or 'Don't forget us!' The
people on the street froze where they stood, horrified.

I didn't shout; I didn't scream. I thought about how crazy
it was that my life was going to end like this. I and everyone
else on the bus knew that as one of the most obvious organisers of the protests at our school I would certainly go to
prison. Most of the other girls stood at least some chance of
being set free after being given a warning, but not me.

I was standing near the back door. The girls around me
started looking at each other, at me and at the door. They
nudged me closer to it. When the bus had to stop at an

intersection they pushed as hard as they could on the doors. No-one said a word. They just looked at each other and pushed. The doors opened enough for me to squeeze through and I jumped out.

I fell onto the road but got to my feet quickly. The soldiers behind the bus stopped their jeep and jumped out. I ran towards a rug shop at the intersection, weaving through buses, cars and shoppers. I made it through the door and said to the shop owner, 'They're going to take me to Pul-i-charki!' Straight away he led me to the back of the shop. It was dimly lit and there were huge Afghani rugs piled on top of each other, rolled up in corners or hanging on the walls. He went to one of the piles at the back, lifted a rug and said, 'Get under.' I lay there still and silent under the thick, heavy rug. A minute or two later I heard one of the soldiers say, 'Did you see a girl? Did a girl come in here?' The shop owner said, 'No, I didn't see any girls.'

I lay there for about an hour until the shop owner told me it was safe to come out; the soldiers had given up. I will never forget the man's face: he had such innocent, kind eyes. For him to hide me was very brave because if the soldiers had found me in his shop he would've gone to prison too. I thanked him, left his shop and started walking towards my bus stop, near school, so I could catch a bus home. I was feeling pretty pleased – I'd escaped going to jail, I was safe, and now I could go home – but also a little nervous about what might happen to me next.

One of my father's brothers, Uncle Khan Mohammed, pulled up in his car beside me and told me to get in. He had an anxious expression on his face and he kept glancing around as though someone might be watching us. Once he'd pulled away from the kerb he told me that he and my father had been out searching for me to make sure I didn't return home. 'Gita's mother informed on you today. They'll be coming for you tonight.'

My happiness at having escaped the bus to Pul-i-charki disappeared and my stomach went cold, as though it had turned to ice. I looked out the car window at people walking down the street doing normal things – shopping, visiting people, walking home from school – and it all seemed unreal.

Uncle Khan Mohammed took me to hide at his house in Khair Khana. He tried to soothe me, saying that he would sort everything out and it would all be okay – so long as I stayed out of sight the police wouldn't find me. My cousins told me not to worry, but I could hear fear and worry in their own voices. The day dragged on into night. And then the days dragged on into weeks. Whenever there was a knock on the door I had to rush to the basement. My Auntie Nafisa, who was one of my father's sisters, grew lots of apples in her garden and stored them in Uncle Khan Mohammed's basement in big boxes. I loved apples, but instead of cheering me up they just made me think of my mother, sisters and brothers, and how much I wished they could eat them with me. My uncle said it was too dangerous for them to come and see me, so I asked one of my cousins to take some apples to them. When she got back she said my mother had been crying.

When Uncle Khan Mohammed came to talk to me one day I got excited – perhaps he was here to tell me it was finally safe to come out of hiding. Instead, he told me that things were the worst they'd ever been outside on the streets. It turned out that the day I was taken into custody at school had been the start of a big crackdown by the regime. Pul-i-charki was overflowing with people the police had rounded up in the last couple of weeks. Several of the girls at my school who, like me, had been especially active in the protests had been sent to prison the day we were put on the buses. The rest had each been charged a 10,000 Afghani good behaviour bond, which was almost half a year's salary. The condition of their release was that they would go to prison if they ever got into trouble again. As a result the demonstrations had almost stopped.

'It's not safe for you in Kabul, Mahboba. They'll find you here eventually. You have to leave Afghanistan,' he said. I hadn't realised, but for months Uncle Khan Mohammed had been making plans to move his family and several members of his extended family to Peshawar in Pakistan. He was paying a man to take the group across the border illegally, and now I would be joining them, too. Hundreds of thousands of Afghanis had gone to Peshawar since the Russian invasion. Most of them lived in terrible refugee camps: rows of tents in the dirt, with no running water or electricity. Many refugees died in the camps of hunger or disease. But we would be staying with Uncle Khan Mohammed in a rented house.

A few days before I was about to leave for Pakistan my

mother and Zarmina came to see me. I hadn't seen them for nearly three weeks. It was hard to think of what to say, knowing that this could be the last time I ever saw them. They couldn't stay long, only ten or so minutes, in case they gave me away. My mother told me how scared she had been the day that I disappeared. That night the soldiers had come to my house and shouted at my father: 'Where is Mahboba?' He'd said, 'I don't have a daughter named Mahboba.' They had persisted, asking him over and over where I was, but he had constantly repeated that he'd never had a daughter by that name.

They had wrecked the entire house, searching through all the cupboards and even pulling the pillows out of the pillowcases to see if there was anything hidden inside. They had dug up the back yard because it was common for the Mujaheddin to have their guns hidden in holes in the ground, but of course they had found nothing.

# Chapter 5

It was early 1982 when I went to Pakistan. The first morning of my journey I woke when it was still dark and packed a few things into a small bag. The other family members I would be travelling with were staying at my uncle's house and they got ready too, all of us with tears in our eyes. My grandmother on my father's side of the family, Bebe Khadijah, at about sixty-five years old, had always led a comfortable life in the city. Aunt Nargas, Uncle Khan Mohammed's wife, was eight months pregnant and had six children with her, all between the ages of one and twelve. One of my father's sisters, my Aunt Nafisa, was travelling with her husband and five of their seven children – the other two had already left Afghanistan. Nafisa's husband's extended family was joining us too: lots of children and babies with their mothers, a few young girls like me, and a few elderly men and women. There were about forty of us all up. Uncle Khan Mohammed was not joining us on our trip – he was going to follow separately later.

Like the other women and girls I put on a bright blue *burqa* which covered me from head to foot. No one could see my eyes, as they were covered by the mesh panel on the front of the *burqa*. On this journey the more unidentifiable we were the better. I had worn a *burqa* a few times before, when we had travelled to areas that weren't as liberal and modern as the city. I'd enjoyed wearing it – I still think of the Afghan blue *burqa* as unique and beautiful. It covers you from the sun, and it's cool because air circulates under it. But that day I didn't get any enjoyment from putting it on because I felt so miserable.

We were driven to a place in the city where there was a bus waiting for us. As I was about to get on the bus my father appeared. He spoke with our guide, a man who made his living by smuggling people out of the country, and a few of my relatives, then he came over to me. I broke down and sobbed. He tried to comfort me and told me that everything would be okay, that I was brave like a lion. And then he handed me an armful of plastic bags, at least fifty of them. I looked at him, puzzled, and he said: 'You keep these, you'll need them.'

I got on the bus and looked out the window, hoping that my mother might come. My house was only five minutes' drive away. She still hadn't come when our guide started the engine and pulled out from the kerb. I knew she would've been forbidden from coming because it was too risky. I was in a state of total despair and didn't think I'd see her ever again. I was shaking, I was so scared.

To the east of Kabul lies one of the world's greatest mountain ranges, the Hindu Kush, which we would have to cross to get to safety in Pakistan. For thousands of years people had crossed the Hindu Kush through the Khyber Pass. We would not be able to, though, because it was filled with Russian and Afghani soldiers.

Our guide wouldn't tell us which way we would be going because there was a chance that we would be pulled over and questioned by soldiers or police and if we got scared we might give ourselves away. If questioned we were to say we were travelling to a wedding in Jalalabad, a city in Afghanistan about a hundred and twenty kilometres east of Kabul.

A couple of hours outside of Kabul the bus stopped and our guide told us that we had to get out and walk the next part of our journey. We had entered a Mujaheddin area. The Russians had moved into an old Afghani army garrison from which they could launch attacks on the freedom fighters, and army snipers were stationed in the lookout towers, ready to shoot should the Mujaheddin try to attack. We would have to make it down the road, past the garrison, without the troops seeing or hearing us. If they did, either they would know we were heading to Pakistan and capture us, or mistake us for Mujaheddin and shoot us.

Our guide told us we were to walk very quietly and quickly in single file, bent right over. There was to be no stopping. The mothers weren't to stop and help their children. If the Russians shot us there was nothing our guide could do to help us, and we were not to stop and help anyone else. We started walking. All I could hear was my panting breath and all I could see were the stones beneath my feet. We had to walk more than a kilometre like this. Amazingly we all made it.

For the next week or so we travelled from village to village, usually on foot. I was so traumatised and terrified that I felt numb – I have flashes of memories of the journey but I can recall very few precise details. I remember that sometimes villagers loaned us their donkeys to ride on for a few kilometres, or even a couple of cars. At first it seemed nice to be released from having to walk, but riding was painful because the paths were rocky and we had no saddles. Being in a car was even worse. We'd have fifteen or so people crammed into one car, with people even jammed into the boot. I always hoped I didn't have to get in first because that meant I'd have the weight of three or four people on top of me. I vomited over and over because the road was so rough and winding – at least now I understood why my father had given me all those plastic bags. Other people vomited too and the smell was horrible. We hadn't bathed since we left Kabul. We cried and shouted, and our guide tried to calm us down by promising that when we crossed the border into Pakistan there would be a bus waiting for us.

As we approached Pakistan I looked back at the desert and the mountains of my country disappearing. Then our guide stopped the car and said, 'Say goodbye to your country; you might never see it again.' I got out of the car and lay down with my face to the ground and said, 'Goodbye, beautiful Afghanistan.' We all cried, even our guide.

Then we got into a bus and headed towards our new lives.

~

When we entered Peshawar, Pakistan, the streets were filled with buses and cars, the footpaths were crowded with people, pollution hung thick in the air and it was unbearably hot. The women we passed on the street wore nothing but black, and most were completely covered except for their eyes. In Afghanistan women could wear whatever they liked and if they chose to completely cover themselves they wore a sky-blue *burqa*. I missed that beautiful blue.

All forty of us went to Uncle Haji's place the first night. I couldn't walk properly and had bruises all over my body, mostly on my arms and legs, but even on my face, probably from collapsing on the ground while we were walking. I had lost a lot of weight and was dehydrated. Every time I ate or drank something, even water, I vomited. I was aching all over so my cousin Nasima, my Uncle Haji's daughter who was a year older than me and used to play with me in Shahr-e-now, gave me a wonderful massage until I fell asleep. The next day I had a shower; after such a long journey it felt good to be clean again.

I stayed a few nights at Uncle Haji's, a couple of months with my Aunt Nafisa, and then my grandmother and

I moved in permanently with my Uncle Khan Mohammed, in a rented house. My grandmother and I slept in the corridor outside the ground floor bedroom where Uncle Khan Mohammed, Aunt Nargas and their six children slept. They offered for us to sleep in their bedroom too but we preferred being out in the corridor where every now and then there was a bit of a breeze. It was summer and the temperature sometimes got to forty-nine degrees.

On the second floor there was one bedroom where another of my father's sisters, my Aunt Gulalai, and her three children lived, and a second room that was always filled with guests visiting Peshawar. On top was a courtyard surrounded by a high concrete wall. That was where I went to see sunshine and breathe fresh air. Kabul girls were attractive to the men in Peshawar because to them we looked fair-skinned, so my uncle didn't want me and my aunts and female cousins to go out unless we were dressed the way the local women were. The weather was so hot and humid that it was nearly impossible to breathe, so we hardly ever went out.

With so many people staying, there were always piles of laundry to do. Every day I helped Aunt Nargas do the washing by hand, just as Zarmina did at home in Kabul. I scrubbed the clothes of the people living in Khan Mohammed's house. I scrubbed the stairs and the floors, too. I wanted to show how grateful I was that my aunt and uncle were letting me live with them in safety, but it was hard to work because I felt weak and depressed. I had headaches every day and couldn't sleep at night. I had survived the journey out of Afghanistan and didn't have to worry about being put in prison or bombed or shot by the Russians any more, but I didn't feel happy. I had forgotten about happiness. When I tried to imagine the future everything looked dark. My Aunt Nargas suffered worse than me. About a month after we arrived in Peshawar she gave birth to a baby boy, but the journey had placed too much stress on him in the womb and he died a couple of days later.

I thought a lot about other Afghani refugees in Peshawar who had to live in tents in refugee camps. All they had to eat was bread and water, and they were exposed to the harsh sun in the summer and the cold in winter, which I was to learn was bitter. The big aid organisations and overseas governments who provided aid did not go directly to the people in the refugee camps, but gave their money to those in power, and it was up to them to distribute the aid to the people who needed it. The refugees received very little. Some people had plenty of good clothes, drove nice cars, lived in big houses and wore gold jewellery – and I knew how many children were dying in the refugee camps.

While I bent over the basin scrubbing clothes at my uncle's place I thought about what I would do if one day I could be in charge of giving out aid to people. I wouldn't distribute it from the top down the way the big aid groups and governments did. I'd go straight to the people at the bottom, to the ones who needed it the most. The little child who hadn't eaten for four days couldn't afford to wait for aid to trickle down to her. I felt so frustrated that I could see a better way but had no power to do anything about it.

We were lucky in that we had a roof over our heads and sometimes had meat to eat because Uncle Khan Mohammed had a job printing photographs. He didn't talk about his job, perhaps because to him it seemed like a step down from the life he'd led in Afghanistan. He'd had a beautiful house in Shahr-e-now, worked in a cinema and owned a Mercedes Benz. He did anything he wanted, and wasn't held back by traditions. He was the only one of my uncles who dressed in a modern way. He liked to have fun and spend money on his friends and on parties, and he had a big peer group who followed and looked up to him. When he became a refugee he lost everything. It wasn't possible for him – or any of the other Afghani refugees – to sell their houses and cars in Afghanistan before they left because as soon as the secret police discovered you were selling up they knew you must be preparing to flee the country. Refugees had to leave everything behind and come to Pakistan empty-handed.

One of the things I had in common with the refugees in the camps was that I was not receiving any education. There were plenty of schools, but because my cousins and I weren't Pakistani citizens we weren't allowed to go. We had to pick up the major language of Pakistan, Urdu, by listening to people speak it. There were quite a few educated women who had become refugees and they had set up some basic reading and writing classes for the younger children in one of the refugee camps. I wanted to go to the camp and help teach but it would have meant taking the bus on my own across Peshawar and my uncle was worried that something might happen to me. He felt that it was his duty to protect me on behalf of my father.

Another thing I had in common with the refugees in the camps was my clothing. I had two outfits, one of which was an orange cotton dress that had come from an aid group. They had distributed one-size-fits-all dresses that were about size twenty-two; on me it looked like a big orange tent. My relatives and I had sewn them up so that they fitted us but I still felt like I was wearing an ugly uniform. I was only a teenager and in my heart I would've loved to have bought nice clothes and jewellery at the bazaar. Some-times my cousins would give me their clothes to wear. I remember a pretty blue dress that Nasima let me wear that made me feel like a girl again.

For me the worst thing about being a refugee was being separated from my family and not knowing whether they were okay. We couldn't call each other on the phone because there were hardly any telephones in Afghanistan, and even if my parents had had access to a phone I wouldn't have called them because of the risk of the line being tapped by the government. We couldn't send letters to each other by mail either. If the government read one of our letters and discovered I had fled to Peshawar my family would be branded anti-government. My family had to pretend that I didn't exist.

The only way we could communicate was through friends and relatives who were travelling to and from

Peshawar. One day I received a visit from a friend of Anwar's. My father had sent word through someone to Anwar in Tehran that I was in Peshawar, and Anwar had asked his friend to deliver some money to me on his next visit to Pakistan. I covered myself and went with my aunts and cousins to a bazaar and bought some clothes for my brothers and sisters. I packaged them up with the rest of the money, about five hundred dollars, and gave it to someone who was travelling to Kabul. It was my way of saying: 'I'm alive, I'm safe, I'm here.'

The first letter I received was from my father. He got someone who was coming to Peshawar to bring it to me by hand. It was a big risk for this man: if he were caught before he reached the border with a letter to a refugee in Peshawar he would be in serious trouble. My heart became lighter when I read that letter. My father wrote that he loved me and missed me; he was very proud of me, his 'sweet lion daughter'.

Back in Kabul, like girls all over the world, I had daydreamed about being a famous singer. My father had forbidden me from singing – according to my culture it wasn't good for women to be singers and many families discouraged their girls from singing. I had sung with my cousin Shakria, who travelled with me from Kabul, when our fathers weren't home, and we had sung at wedding and engagement parties – but only in front of the women, not the men.

Months before we escaped Kabul, Shakria and I had recorded a tape of us singing, and had kept it hidden from our fathers. One of the songs we had sung, which was very popular at the time, was about the heartache of having to leave Afghanistan. Part of it translates something like this:

We are going from your sight, oh my friend, goodbye.
With a heart full of hope we are going, oh my friend, goodbye.
With eyes full of tears we are going, oh my friend, goodbye.

Because so many people were fleeing the country a lot of the popular songs during the Russian regime were about leaving and being separated from family. Shakria and I recording this song was our way of saying goodbye. We, like all Afghanis, felt that we would be leaving our homeland eventually, we just didn't know exactly when.

Days before we were about to leave Kabul for Peshawar we took the tape out of its hiding place and gave it to one of our cousins to give to my mother. She must have played it to my father. I would have expected him to lecture me in his letter about disobeying him by singing, but as I read on I started to smile: he wrote that he thought my voice was beautiful, and that it was good to hear the sound of it again.

# Chapter 6

After I'd been in Peshawar for a few months Anwar came to live with me at Uncle Khan Mohammed's. He had escaped to Iran as a refugee without the proper papers so he had to travel by land; he'd had a longer and more dangerous journey than mine. It was wonderful to see him again and to know I had a brother who cared about me so much he would risk his life to come and look after me, but I felt guilty. Anwar had worked hard to make a comfortable life for himself in Tehran, and now had given up his job and home for me. He moved into the guest room upstairs. With the money he'd made in Iran he opened a grocery store.

One of Omar's best friends, Assad, had been in Peshawar for a few months. They were as close as brothers, and Assad was close to one of my male cousins, too. He was considered like a part of our family. Assad had been worried about being conscripted into the army, so he'd fled to Peshawar. A few months after he arrived he fell ill and ended up in hospital in a coma. The doctors feared he might die. He had no family in Peshawar – they were scattered between Iran, Afghanistan and Australia.

I remembered Assad as being quietly spoken and polite, and very respectful. He had an innocence about him. It was sad to hear my family in Peshawar discussing what they should do if he died: bury him here in Pakistan or send his body back home.

Assad eventually came out of his coma, but he remained seriously ill. For the next three months one of my cousins spent every day at the hospital with him. He helped him to get to the bathroom and the toilet. He brought him fresh clothes each day and took his dirty ones back for me to wash. The hospital food was bad so every day he took in food for him cooked by my Aunt Rona, and helped him to eat. At night he even slept on the floor beside his bed.

Finally Assad's condition improved enough that he could leave hospital. Then my cousin who had looked after him in hospital asked me to help find a wife for him. Assad was in his mid to late twenties and ready to marry. I asked several girls who I thought would make suitable brides but they all said no straight away because they had heard about his sickness. Traditionally, girls only wanted men who they were sure could support them because there was no health care or social security and women were expected to stay at home and raise children, not work to support the family.

Assad often went to visit my Aunt Nafisa. One day I happened to be there when he visited. I was upstairs and when I came back down I saw him sitting on the floor chatting with my aunt. I hadn't seen him since Kabul. I sat down and joined the conversation for a few minutes then excused myself and left.

A few weeks later, one of my cousins handed me an envelope and said it was from Assad. I ripped it open in excitement, thinking that Assad probably had some news about my family in Afghanistan to share with me. But I soon realised that this was no ordinary letter. He wrote about the day he had seen me at Aunt Nafisa's, about how when he saw me coming down the stairs he wondered whether I was really a girl or in fact an angel. He said he wanted to marry me.

I was stunned. I had never thought of Assad in that way at all. I had never really thought about any boys in that way. Even though I was in my mid-teens and considered old enough for marriage, it was the last thing on my mind. My surprise turned to anxiety in an instant. Sending a letter like this was strictly forbidden. In Afghani culture it is wrong for a man to directly approach a girl; he should speak with her father or other male relatives. Assad knew that if he did they would immediately refuse his proposal: my family had helped and supported him as if he were one of us, so now he was like a brother to me and they would feel that he had no right to look on me as a wife. They loved and trusted him – and he had gone behind their backs. There could be terrible consequences.

I wrote a short letter back to him. I told him that I thought of him like a brother. I had six brothers and I considered him the seventh. I said that I was worried about what would happen if my family found out he felt this way and that he had sent me a letter. They would see it as a betrayal of the trust they had put in him. I gave it to my cousin to give to Assad.

A couple of days later one of my cousins arrived with the news that Assad was back in hospital. I felt terrible; I was sure it was the shock of my rejection that had made him sick again.

That night I had a terrible dream. I was on a crowded Peshawar street. It was a foggy day. Assad was staggering through the crowd. He had his hands stretched out in front of him and was saying, 'Help me, help me,' but everyone was walking straight past, ignoring him. He looked weak, as though he was about to collapse. I ran to him, only my feet didn't touch the ground – I was flying to him. I grabbed his hand just before he was about to fall.

When I woke up I was shaking. It was the middle of the night. I went into the bedroom and got one of my female cousins up and told her about my dream. She said, 'It doesn't mean anything, go back to sleep.' I went back to my bed in the hallway and prayed for guidance about my dream till the sun came up.

The next day I couldn't get Assad out of my thoughts. He had a gentle, respectful manner. And now that I thought about it, he was on the handsome side. He was starting to look less like a brother to me. I had been looking for a wife for Assad but perhaps my real role in life was to be his wife myself.

I wrote a letter to Assad wishing that he get better soon. The cousin who had delivered the other letters took it to Assad in hospital and brought another back to me from him. He wrote that I shouldn't worry: receiving my letter had made him so happy that he would certainly recover. He did, and was out of hospital in a couple of days.

Shortly after that I received another letter from Assad, and realised that he had taken my 'get well' letter as a 'yes'. Over the next few months we continued to exchange letters, mostly delivered by my cousin, who never suspected that we were discussing marriage – he thought that we were sharing news about my family in Afghanistan.

I saw Assad briefly every now and then when I visited my aunt's house and he happened to be there. We never really got a chance to speak, though. Instead we shared our thoughts on paper, getting to know each other the only way possible. Our letters were innocent – not at all what you would call love letters. We wrote about the things that were happening in our day-to-day lives, our worries for our families in Kabul, how we felt about being refugees. And I wrote about how worried I was that Omar would be upset and disappointed in me when he found out that we had been secretly writing letters to each other. After all, the two men were best friends.

For the first time since I had arrived in Peshawar the blackness that I'd carried around with me started to lift. I began to feel alive again. Living as a refugee, far from my

immediate family, I was lonely, and now I had found someone I could share my thoughts with.

I wrote to tell Assad that I would marry him. He wrote
back that he would ask my family for my hand in marriage.
We exchanged letters about the best way of breaking it to
my family. My relationship with Omar was really important
to me so we decided that Assad should first talk to Omar,
then Omar would tell the rest of the family.

Fear and guilt jolted me at times: according to my culture
I shouldn't even have been accepting Assad's letters, let alone
writing back promising to marry him. I couldn't stop myself,
though. All my joy in life depended on the next letter arriving
from him. I would hide on the roof late at night to write my
letters and give them to my cousin to pass on.

I hid all of Assad's letters in a big green khaki bag that one
of my cousins had given me to store my things in – I tucked
them in amongst my clothes. Some of Anwar's and my
cousins' clothes and documents were stored in the bag, too,
and it hung on the wall in the corridor where I slept at night.
I knew it was dangerous to hide the letters there but I had
nowhere else to put them. I didn't want to throw them away
because I planned to send them to Omar eventually, to
prove how innocent we were. Anyone who read the letters
could see that.

≈

I knew something was up as soon as I walked through the
door after spending a couple of hours at Uncle Haji's. The

house was too quiet, and everyone looked too worried. I ran to check the khaki bag. All the letters were gone. I felt sick. My family had trusted me a hundred percent and had never suspected that I would get involved with a man behind their backs – especially Assad, who they had treated like a son and brother.

No-one talked about what I had done but the atmosphere was different – quiet and tense. I tried to pass the time as though everything was normal – I did the laundry, scrubbed the floors, looked after my little cousins – but inside I was dying. I couldn't eat or sleep and I jumped every time there was a sound at the door. I didn't hear anything from Assad; it was dreadful not knowing if he was okay. I felt so alone, without my mother or Zarmina to ask for advice. Back in Kabul I didn't have a very strong relationship with my grandmother. I respected her as my grandmother but that was all – until I got to know her in Pakistan. We lay next to each other on our mattresses in the corridor at night, unable to get to sleep, and chatted to each other in whispers. It was highly unusual in Afghani society to talk to your grandmother about your personal life, but we had grown so close that now I talked to her about Assad. She was very supportive and sympathetic; she didn't punish me or show any anger towards me.

The word spread through my extended family. They had trusted me so much and never imagined I would get involved with a boy, and when they found out the truth they were devastated. Most believed that Assad had betrayed the family and must never be allowed to marry me. Uncle Haji tried to calm everyone down, reminding them that we had only exchanged letters. 'Mahboba didn't go to the movies with him, or do anything bad.'

Anwar was in one of Pakistan's big cities, Karachi, on business when the letters were found. When he returned no-one was talking openly about what had happened but he could tell from everyone's behaviour that something wasn't right. He asked me what was wrong. I told him I didn't know. When someone finally told him what I had done he stared into my eyes and said, 'Is this true?' I nodded yes. Without saying another word he turned and walked out of the house. He was so angry that he didn't come home that night.

I had hurt my family. My reputation was destroyed. I would never be able to hold my head up again. Some of my relatives were no longer speaking to me. A doctor had prescribed Valium to help me sleep. I swallowed a bottleful of the tablets and lay down on my bed at about seven in the evening.

I was starting to drift away when my Aunt Nargas came to find me. Her concerned, anxious face flickered in and out of my vision as she bent over me. I couldn't keep my eyes open. She ran from the room, shouting. The next thing I knew one of my cousins was lifting me up in his arms and putting me over his shoulder. My body felt heavy and loose. Suddenly we were out on the footpath. I saw a car pull up. And then everything faded out.

$\sim$

When I woke up the next morning I didn't know where I was. My Aunt Nargas was sitting near me, looking worried and exhausted. She got up, took my hand and told me I was in hospital. A doctor had pumped out my stomach, then she had sat by my bedside all night.

I came home from hospital feeling even more depressed and ashamed than before. When Anwar returned home his attitude had softened. He felt that even though I had made a mistake, there was no reason to turn it into a big drama and make me feel as bad as some of my family were doing. He agreed with Uncle Haji that we had only exchanged letters. Having Anwar back at home and being supportive of me made me feel like I could go on with life.

Assad had left Peshawar. I was miserable but most of my family were relieved. I was never punished. I guess that losing the friendship and respect of many of my family members was punishment enough.

∾

My Uncle Khan Mohammed always had lots of guests staying and one week there was a wealthy man visiting from Dubai in the United Arab Emirates. He kept asking me to do little favours for him, like washing his socks and ironing his shirts. I liked him so I did everything he asked without any complaints. After he'd left, my Aunt Gulalai came and said that he had come to visit to see whether I would make a good wife for his son. He had been impressed with the way I had behaved all week and had proposed. My aunt handed me the boy's photograph. She said his father was extremely wealthy and had offered to take me, my mother and all my brothers and sisters to live in Dubai, an oil city known for its high standard of living. I wouldn't have to be a refugee any more. I would live in luxury.

'Go to Dubai, Mahboba. Have children and forget about Assad,' she said. I shook my head. 'But don't you want to live a comfortable life?'

'I never want to be wealthy,' I said. 'Please tell this man that I'm sorry, I can't marry his son.' I gave her back the photo – I hadn't even glanced at it.

# Chapter 7

I heard nothing from Assad after he disappeared from Peshawar. My grandmother said, 'He's left you. He is not coming back.' I lost interest in the world. I lost interest even in living. I told Anwar that there was no other man for me than Assad; I wouldn't marry anyone else.

Then, after six months of silence, one of Assad's brothers who lived in Australia, Ehsan, contacted Omar and told him that Assad had moved to Australia with him. Ehsan had applied for him to get a permanent residency visa on the grounds of family reunion. He had been granted it around the time that the letters had been found, and had gone to Australia as soon as he could. Assad had not forgotten me, Ehsan said. He still wanted to marry me. It turned out that I had nothing to fear from Omar's reaction: he wasn't angry. Omar and Ehsan wanted to help and they discussed the options. It was impossible for us to get married in Pakistan because there was too much opposition from my family in Peshawar – but if I could get across the border into India we would be free to. They decided to ask Anwar whether he would take me there.

When Anwar came and asked me if I would like to go to India with him so I could marry Assad it was a happy day for me, even though I knew we would have a very difficult journey ahead of us. Unlike the Afghanistan–Pakistan border, which in places was unguarded, the border with India was very strictly controlled. It wasn't just because refugees like us were trying to cross but because since Pakistan and India had been partitioned after the Second World War battles had been fought along the border over who should control Kashmir.

It would be hard to get through the border checks because, like nearly all Afghani refugees, we didn't have passports or visas. We had no identity; it was as if we didn't exist according to the law. Probably many thousands of Afghani refugees have died without anybody being aware, because there was no numbering or identification system. We had no paperwork, no photographs, no value. If either the Pakistanis or Indians found that we were in their country illegally we would end up in jail for years – or be shot and killed.

We would need far more money than we'd had when we escaped from Afghanistan, because we would have to bribe border guards and immigration officials. The Afghani guide who had taken me to Pakistan had charged my uncle lots of money and had put a lot of pressure on us to complete our journey quickly, but the Pakistani and Indian officials would be different. They would feel nothing towards us.

I had heard many stories of terrible things happening to Afghani people crossing the border into India but I felt that I had lived through worse escaping from Afghanistan, so when Anwar asked me if I wanted to go I didn't hesitate in saying yes. And Anwar sacrificed himself for me again. After building up his business over the previous couple of years, he sold his shop so we could afford to make the journey. We told my relatives in Peshawar that we were going to India – but not the reason.

First we drove a couple of hours to Lahore, a town on the Pakistani side of the border. Anwar hired a car and we went with a big group of Afghanis – all men, except me. Uncle Khan Mohammed came with us. I told him that he didn't need to, that he should stay home, but he had looked after me in Peshawar for the past couple of years and he couldn't let me go without ensuring I was okay. We spent a couple of nights in a hotel, Anwar busy making arrangements to get us across the border.

I was nervous about the first part of our journey: we had to pass through an immigration check at a gate in a big wall, and there were many soldiers stationed at the gate. Sometimes Afghanis tried to climb the wall but they usually got shot. Uncle Khan Mohammed promised to spend the night in Lahore so that if something happened to us while we were trying to cross the border he'd hear about it. Otherwise, if we got shot or imprisoned it might be a long time before our family found out what had happened to us. Our uncle would keep us company as we approached the gate, but once we had entered the gate we would be on our own – he would be powerless to help us. We said our goodbyes. I was really grateful for all that Uncle Khan Mohammed had done for me; he had looked after me like I was a daughter for over two years.

It was terrifying passing through the gate, but it was only the beginning. We had to walk along a long, dusty road through the no-man's land between Pakistan and India, and every so often there was a checkpoint with soldiers and immigration officials. As we approached each check-point I could feel my heart beating – *boom, boom, boom* – knowing that we would be stopped by soldiers with guns who would ask for money in return for letting us pass through without any paperwork.

At one checkpoint Anwar told me to stay where I was and walked off with an immigration official. I was scared about what would happen to us if the man didn't agree to let us through. We wouldn't be able to go back and we wouldn't be able to go forward: we had already broken the law by coming this far. Anwar handed the man a bundle of cash. It was almost all of his life savings; he had kept only a little in his pocket for the rest of our journey. The man wanted more and Anwar said to him in the local language, Urdu, 'I don't have any more. That's it, that's all I have.' He allowed us to move on to the next stage, but we knew that he wasn't happy and probably wouldn't highly recommend us to the next officials we would have to deal with.

We had to join a queue to have our bags searched. We had a couple of changes of clothes and two blankets, and Anwar had a watch, a Walkman and some books. He loved his books. He had left most of them in Peshawar so that one day he could go back and get them, but he had packed some of them into a bag, even though they were very heavy to carry. We knew they wouldn't be interested in his books, but they'd love to get their hands on the Walkman because it was a good-quality foreign-made one that Anwar had got in Iran. If they found it they would surely take it from us. I hid the Walkman in the clothes I was wearing.

At checkpoints that followed border guards asked for more money and my brother gave the last of his cash to them. When all his cash was gone he gave them his watch. At the last checkpoint, a guard asked him for his leather jacket. And that's when he got mad. 'All my money is gone. I am not going to give you anything else,' shouted Anwar. I was really frightened that if he got mad the border guards would decide they'd had enough of us.

They didn't care that Anwar had already given away his life savings to the other guards and immigration officials – they could still shoot him or put him in jail for being an illegal. The guard told me to go through the checkpoint. Suddenly I was on the Indian side of the border, on my own. He told Anwar that unless he wanted to leave me stranded he'd better hand over his jacket.

I said, 'Please, brother, give him the jacket. Don't leave me alone here.'

He shouted at me in Dari so the man couldn't

understand: 'Look, don't worry. I know he's just trying to rip us off. He's going to let me go. Don't cry.'

'I'm going to give him your Walkman,' I said.

'No! No more. You'll give him that Walkman over my dead body,' said Anwar.

Uncle Khan Mohammed had given me some money – equal to a couple of hundred Australian dollars – in case of an emergency. I had said, 'I won't need it, Uncle. Anwar has got a lot of money,' but he had insisted. I hadn't told Anwar about the money – I was saving it in case we went hungry in the future.

I pulled the money from my bag and begged the man: 'Here is the money. This is all we have. Please, let my brother go. I can't leave without my brother.'

He took the money out of my hand and waved Anwar through.

We were both on the Indian side of the border, but we didn't have a cent. Uncle Khan Mohammed had given us the address of his close friend Hakim, who we had met when he stayed with us in Peshawar for three months. Hakim lived in New Delhi, the capital of India, a twelve-hour drive from where we were. We were in a small border town and lots of people who had recently crossed the border were still there, deciding what to do next.

We wandered around and after a while we saw a group of Afghani men who looked very relaxed and well off – they weren't shaking and traumatised like us. Anwar went over and introduced himself. He told them that we had no money but needed to get to New Delhi. They said that we would have to wait until the next day. The conflict over Kashmir had recently flared up and we might get shot if we travelled at night. They invited us to spend the night in their motel; in the morning they would give us the money to get to New Delhi.

On the way to the motel Anwar discovered that the men were wealthy drug dealers who regularly crossed the border with opium grown in Afghanistan. Anwar told me he was worried that if we stayed the night with them and they were caught with drugs the police would arrest us too. Once I was inside my room I prayed that the night would go quickly. Because we had had such a long and frightening walk across the border I slept very well, and in the morning one of the men gave us enough money to pay someone to drive us to New Delhi.

We were happy to see Hakim and grateful that he let us stay with him. We would be able to look after ourselves as soon as we got some money together. But after only a week or so Hakim asked us to leave. He and his wife had two young sons and he felt that it wasn't convenient to have us staying there. I could hardly believe that Hakim wanted us to leave when we didn't have any money.

Anwar had no option but to sell his books: the books that he had held on to in Iran for almost twenty years, then carried from Iran to Pakistan, and across the border into India. He had a lot of trouble finding somewhere we could afford to live, but finally he found a place and paid a month's bond and a month's rent. It was a third-floor flat that had been empty for a long time. It was terribly hot up there but we were excited and happy that we had managed to find a place. We moved in. All we had were our clothes, Anwar's Walkman and two blankets.

Anwar had a rupee left so he went and bought us a loaf of bread. We ate, and laid our blankets on the ground to sleep. I put my bag under my head like a pillow and covered myself in my prayer shawl. The next day we finished the bread. We drank water straight from the tap – it smelt bad and looked dirty. Anwar went out to think about what to do, but he came back looking hopeless.

We spent four days without food. We became weak, until on the fourth day I couldn't walk over and stand at the tap to drink. Anwar and I had never begged in our lives; we would rather die than go begging. We heard a samosa vendor out on the street, yelling that it was only half a rupee for four samosas. Anwar said, 'Hang on a minute,' and pulled a half-rupee coin from his pocket. He left as fast as he could to catch him. He returned with the samosas and we ate two each. They were full of chilli. After four days with nothing in our stomachs except bad tap water it was the worst thing we could've eaten. We felt really sick and had bad pains in our stomachs.

On the fifth day there was a knock on our door. When we moved in we had said hello to five or six young Afghani men who lived on the first floor. They hadn't seen us coming and going from the building so they were worried about what had happened to us. When they saw the state we were in they went straight downstairs to their flat and brought us back plates piled high with rice and meat and bread. They were refugees, too, but they had been in New Delhi for some time and had jobs and small incomes.

After we had finished eating, one of the men said to Anwar, 'Now you've eaten your food, come downstairs. We need to talk with you about something.'

Anwar left and was gone for quite some time. I knew something serious was going on. When he returned he said, 'We have to move from this house straight away.'

I said, 'What? We just paid bond and a month's rent.'

'Don't ask me too many questions. We can't stay in this flat. I'm going out for the rest of the day; give me the Walkman. I have to sell it so we can move as soon as possible. Don't go outside, don't open the door to anybody, don't go on the balcony.'

For four days we'd been lying on the floor like we were dead. Now we had food, and people were looking out for us. They'd said they would bring us breakfast, lunch and dinner until we had some money. I was happy. I wanted to go outside for a walk.

Anwar said, 'Don't! Don't even answer the door if someone knocks. You'll know when it's me because I'll call out to you.'

I said 'Okay,' and he left. I hadn't even tried to ask him what was going on, but I knew it must be something serious if he was selling the Walkman. I sat inside on my own all day. After it had gotten dark, around seven-thirty, there was a knock on the door. I thought it was probably Anwar so I walked over and said 'Who is it?' Anwar didn't answer. No-one answered. I thought, maybe the men

downstairs have brought us some food. Because my brother wasn't home, according to my culture they couldn't
come and talk to me – they would knock and leave the
plate for me by the door.

There was a bolt on the door, up the top. I slid it down
and opened the door a crack to see if there was any food
there. There were six young Indian men, all drunk, on the
other side of the door. They were saying things to me in
Hindi and pushing against the door, trying to get it open.
With all my power I pushed back. I nearly had the door
closed and they pushed it open again; I nearly got it closed
and they pushed it open again. Open and closed, open and
closed. I screamed in Dari to the Afghani men downstairs
to come and help me. My arms were trembling trying to
fight the strength of the Indian men. Finally I got it closed
and slid the bolt in. I put my back to the door and started
to cry. They pounded on the door. I thought they were
going to bash it down and rape me. I stood there, feeling
nothing, my mind blank, waiting for whatever would
happen next.

I heard the Afghani men run up from the downstairs
flat. There was a lot of scuffling and shouting. It sounded
like they had grabbed the Indian men and were taking them
downstairs. There was no more knocking, no more
shouting; it was all quiet out in the corridor. I slid down to
sit on the floor, leaning against the door. I remember
thinking how tired I was of everything.

After an hour or so there was a knock at the door and
I heard Anwar's voice: 'Open the door, it's me.' I wouldn't

open it at first. He said, 'Mahboba, it's okay. Open the door, it's me.' Finally I let him in.

He explained that our flat had been a brothel. Men who didn't realise the prostitutes had moved away continued to visit the address – that's why no-one had wanted to rent it.

The next day we tried to get our money back from the landlord but he wouldn't give it to us. Instead, the Afghani men on the ground floor gave us the same amount; they said that they'd find some men to move in, who could then pay them back. The kindness of those men meant so much to us when we had nothing.

Anwar felt it would be quicker for him to look for a new place to live if he was on his own so he wanted to leave me to sit somewhere safe and wait for him, but I refused. I didn't want to be on my own. He shouted at me to stay behind but I didn't care; I just kept following him.

We were in a poor area of New Delhi, walking along the footpath, not really knowing where we were going. A white limousine passed us, stopped and reversed. Anwar was annoyed because it stirred up a lot of dust. I heard a voice calling 'Zalmay, Zalmay', which is Anwar's nickname. The car stopped and a man got out. He was probably about thirty, with beautifully styled hair that was just starting to go silver. He was like an angel walking towards us. He and Anwar hugged each other.

The man's name was Khaled. A friend of Uncle Khan Mohammed, he also knew Anwar. He happened to be driving past on his way somewhere. He invited us to stay at his house, picked up my bag and offered me the front seat of the car. We drove from this very poor area to a beautiful suburb with big houses and gardens. The suburb was full of Afghani refugees, but well-off refugees who had been in India for a while and had established businesses or got good jobs. Khaled made his living by importing goods from Europe that were hard to come by in India.

Khaled lived with his mother, brothers and sisters in a lovely, huge house. Khaled's family was wonderful – full of love. His mother was the greatest comfort I had found since leaving Afghanistan. Straight away I asked her, 'Do you mind if I call you Mother?'

She said, 'Not at all, because you are my sweet daughter.'

After we had been there a few days Anwar went out looking for a house for us to rent. Khaled's mother wanted us to live with them, but we didn't want to put the family to any more trouble. I had become good friends with Khaled's brother, Rahim, who was the funniest man in the world to me, always making jokes to try to make me happy. He said that he knew of a place for rent that might be within our budget. We couldn't afford much. He took me to a house down the road that had a 'For Rent' sign on it and we knocked on the door. An old Indian woman answered. She showed us the property that was for rent: it was actually the garage. The old lady lived in the house with her son, his wife and their three children.

I liked the old lady. She had a friendly, smiling face and I felt safe with her. And the house was within walking distance of Khaled's house so I could easily visit. I didn't know if Anwar would accept living in a garage but I agreed to rent it without even discussing it with him. I told the old woman we would move in the next day.

Anwar was taken aback at first when he saw that the place I had rented for us was a garage. Most days he was out, though. I said, 'You're out all the time. I'm the one who'll be in the garage all day.'

He said, 'Well, if you're happy, I'm happy.'

About a week after we moved in we received a letter from Omar. He wrote to say that Assad's mother and sister had gone to my father in Kabul to officially propose for me to marry Assad, and Assad's brother Ehsan was coming to visit us in New Delhi to organise the engagement and wedding. Once we were married I would go and join Assad in Australia.

I was overjoyed. Now I knew there was a future for me. I'd got what I really wanted: to marry Assad. I couldn't wait for Ehsan to come.

When Assad's family went to my father to propose for me he rejected their proposal and asked them to leave his house. They told him that Assad and I were determined and nothing was going to stop us from getting married – they had come to propose to my father only out of respect for him and Afghani tradition. My father thought Assad wasn't good enough for me. He told them that he would never give his permission or blessing for our marriage. My mother told me many years later that my father was so upset I was going to marry Assad that for a month or so he couldn't sleep and spent his nights pacing in the back yard, and he often cried.

~

Anwar wanted me to learn a skill I could use in Australia and he enrolled me in a six-month sewing course with a group of Afghani women. He thought it would make me happy to go out and meet people and learn something. But I hated it. I cried because I was so bad at sewing. If we had to make a dress for an assignment, by the time it was due everybody else had a dress to hand in to the teacher except me. I couldn't even cut the fabric properly let alone sew it. The other women – many of whom went on to become tailors – encouraged me but it was hopeless.

I had to catch a bus to get to the sewing school. Buses are incredibly crowded in India and you have to stand squashed up against other people. I didn't mind having to touch other women, but according to my religion I could not allow a strange man to touch me. At first, Anwar caught the bus with me each day, pushing people out of the way so I could get on and off. Usually we missed one or two stops because it took us so long to get out. And Anwar got into fights with a few men who couldn't understand why he was pushing them out of the way.

After a week or so of catching the bus Anwar bought a bicycle. I'd never been on one before. Anwar pedalled and I sat in front of him or behind him but I had trouble keeping my balance, so Anwar had trouble keeping his balance, and then we ended up fighting. The traffic was terrible and people were always blowing their horns at us. I only lasted a few weeks at the sewing classes anyway. I asked Anwar if I could stop because I knew I was never going to get any better at it.

It was very dark in the garage because there were no windows and after what had happened in the flat I didn't like to have the garage door open when I was home alone. The only time I opened it was when Anwar came home. We didn't have a TV; we didn't even have the Walkman any more. We had two folding beds, some pillows, a pressure cooker, and cups and plates.

We didn't have much, but the three months we spent living in that garage were one of the happiest periods in my life. I felt like I had a future to look forward to. The old woman made me feel loved. She spent hours teaching me to speak Hindi. She took me shopping and showed me where to buy all the best ingredients. Each morning at four o'clock she woke me up to take me to the Hindu temple where she worshipped. I didn't start practising her religion but I watched the colourful rituals and listened to the beautiful music. For years I hadn't had the chance to relax and simply enjoy something. Every morning the ceremony calmed and refreshed me. I didn't stop loving my own religion, but I found the Hindu temple fascinating. When we got home each morning I did my own prayers.

It is a custom in parts of India to show your close friendship to someone by giving them a bracelet of woven string.

I felt like I had truly become part of the family when the old woman's son, who did not have a sister, came and gave me one of these bracelets. He said he considered me his sister. Some nights I would sit inside the house with the whole family watching Indian movies.

But shortly before Ehsan was due to arrive we had to move, because it wasn't suitable to have him staying in the garage with us. My father had found a girl named Shahla who was living in Afghanistan that he thought Anwar might like to marry. He had sent Anwar her photo and told him that she was a good woman. Anwar had agreed to marry her, and so my father was making wedding arrangements. Shahla's uncle, Habib, and his wife, Mary, and their two children lived in New Delhi, so Anwar and I went to meet them several times. Habib and Mary were full of life. They laughed a lot, and were obviously very much in love with each other. They were an outgoing and carefree couple. And Mary was a good cook. She made beautiful Afghani sweets that I hadn't tasted since I'd left my mother. Anwar and Habib found a nice house and we all moved in together.

It was really upsetting for my Indian mother and my Indian brother when I moved out. I cried when I left them because even though I had only known them for three months it had been an important time for me, a time when I felt I was truly beginning to live my life.

# Chapter 8

Anwar had been close friends with Assad's brother Ehsan since they'd met in Iran ten years earlier, and they took up their friendship where they had left off. I immediately liked Ehsan. He was twenty-six years old and a beautiful human being – very honest and caring. Straight away I felt like he was one of my brothers and I trusted him totally.

Ehsan had friends in New Delhi and sometimes he would take me out with them to see Indian movies or have dinner. He loved music and he got me to sing popular Dari songs with him; I was impressed by his huge collection of tapes of various singers. India meant a lot to Ehsan. He loved everything about the country and the people, the culture and the movies. He planned to live and work there for a year after I had married Assad and moved to Australia.

We quickly became close friends. There were many times when we talked until four in the morning – until Anwar shouted: 'Shut up both of you. I want to sleep. What can you talk about all night?' Ehsan was very open and talked about anything with me: the music he loved, what it was like to live in Australia, his family, his past – nothing was secret.

He told me the most beautiful words that I had ever heard from anybody, about how happy he was that I was marrying Assad. He said I would bring joy to his whole family, and promised me that for as long as he was my brother-in-law he would never let anything happen to make me unhappy. He made me feel good about myself.

Ehsan's first job in arranging my marriage to Assad was organising an engagement party. First, we had to buy an engagement ring. Ehsan and Mary took me to jewellery stores and showed me many rings. Looking back, I can't believe how I reacted. When you're a teenage girl you're supposed to want jewellery but after everything that had happened over the previous few years I was no longer attracted to it. I liked to dress plainly and I didn't wear make-up. I kept saying, 'No, I don't need this.' Partly I was worried about spending money. I was thinking poor, even though Ehsan had brought money from Australia. He found it fascinating: a young girl who didn't want to buy anything. Finally, Mary managed to get me to buy a ring.

Anwar bought me an outfit to wear to my engagement party: a soft, pink cotton top and long skirt. It was nothing fancy, but it was what I wanted. Mary took me to the beautician to have my hair and make-up done. I asked them to put the make-up on so lightly that people didn't even think I was wearing make-up. I covered my face with a scarf all the way home because I thought everybody was looking at me. Mary said, 'Come on, nobody's looking at you.'

The engagement party was at home, with about fifty people from the Afghani community in New Delhi. Anwar bought a tray of colourful sweets and gave them to Ehsan – it was a traditional way to officially accept Assad's proposal. Ehsan put the engagement ring on my finger on Assad's behalf. I was very happy that night and was glad that I chose the ring – it was beautiful. Everyone clapped and Anwar took a few photos. I remember how happy he looked. He was full of life, making jokes. Mary had cooked a lot of delicious food and everyone ate and danced and enjoyed the night.

~

As well as arranging my marriage to Assad, while he was in India Ehsan wanted to find a wife himself, and I wanted to help him. One day he pulled a calendar out of his bag. Each month had a picture of a pretty Afghani girl on it. He asked me which of the girls in the calendar I would choose as his potential bride. I looked through the calendar and picked the girl who I thought looked the most beautiful. Ehsan was really happy that I had chosen her. He said, 'Excellent, your choice is excellent. This is the kind of woman I would like to marry.'

I looked for a wife for him in the supermarket, the shopping centre, everywhere I went. Once a month, Afghani refugees went to the United Nations headquarters to receive a small allowance. One time when I was standing in the queue, a girl caught my eye. She was probably about seventeen, around the same age as me, but much more beautiful. She had a lovely face with long, curly eyelashes, and she had a modern way of dressing.

I went over and spoke with her and her family. The girl was polite and shy, yet very modern-looking. I asked them where they lived and later I went with Mary to visit them. When we got home we described the girl to Ehsan and he thought she sounded nice. When you're proposing on behalf of someone, you need to go a few times. Mary and I went to visit again, and this time we set a date the next week for Ehsan to come and meet the girl and her family.

Ehsan often rode Anwar's bike to visit his friends, Mosen and his wife Soheila, who lived in another part of New Delhi. He liked riding the bike, even though the traffic was very bad and he had enough money to hire a taxi. When people came from Australia they were sick of being in a car.

The night before he was to meet the girl he had a party to go to at his friends' place. He was going to ride over and spend the night there, and return in the morning. I didn't want him to go, in case he missed our appointment with the girl. I begged him not to go: 'Please don't go tonight. Tomorrow is too important.'

'I have to go – my friends will be disappointed. I promise

you I'll be home in time for breakfast.'

In the morning I cooked all of Ehsan's favourite breakfast things and waited for him to come home. I was excited:
this was an important day. When he still hadn't arrived at
nine o'clock I asked Anwar to go and see if he could find
him. We weren't due at the girl's house until one-thirty that
afternoon. Anwar said, 'It's still early, don't worry.'

Mary said jokingly, 'If you're like this with your brother-
in-law, how are you going to be towards your husband?'

'Well, I'm worried about him,' I said. 'He told me he'd
be home for breakfast, and once he's promised me something he doesn't let me down.'

'Maybe his friends just wanted him to have breakfast
with them. He's coming; don't you be silly,' she said.

I got dressed into the clothes I was going to wear when
we went to visit the girl. I sat around waiting. At about
eleven-thirty Ehsan's friend Soheila arrived at our house.
She normally never covered herself with a *burqa* or scarf,
but she had covered her hair with a white scarf – the kind
you usually wear when you are in mourning. Her eyes
were red. Anwar said, 'I am going out.' People from
the Afghani community started arriving. They put long
Afghani mattresses all over the living room floor and
sat down.

'Ehsan always has breakfast with me. Tell me what
happened. Where is he?' I asked.

Someone said, 'He had an accident. He's in hospital, but
he's alive. Don't ask anything else.'

'Take me to the hospital, I want to see him.'

'Just wait for your brother to get back to take you.' They were treating me like a child.

I waited for Anwar to return, but when he did he was being carried by two other men. He couldn't walk.

I grabbed him and shook him and said, 'What's going on? What's wrong with you?'

'Nothing,' he said, 'nothing, I'm okay.' The men laid him on his bed.

Finally, Soheila told me the truth – they couldn't keep it from me any longer. Ehsan had been riding home on his bicycle to come to breakfast when a drunk driver hit him. Ehsan had died instantly. Anwar had gone to identify him at the hospital, and as soon as he'd seen him he collapsed and hadn't been able to walk since. The drunk driver had killed two other people in the same accident.

I became like a crazy woman. I started hitting myself. I hit anyone who came close to me. I banged my head on the wall. I had known Ehsan for only three weeks but they had been an intense three weeks and I had never felt such a close bond of friendship with someone. I owed him everything: he had made my engagement to Assad a reality. Together we had dreamed of his own engagement; we were young and hopeful for the future. I cried, I shouted, I screamed, I pushed people. Nobody could calm me down.

'I don't believe you. He is alive, there's nothing wrong with him. You'd better take me so I can see he's not alive,' I kept saying.

Eventually Soheila's husband, Mosen, agreed to drive me

to the hospital so I could see with my own eyes that Ehsan was dead. We were lucky that his body had even been found. When people die in the street in India it is not like it is here. The population is so much bigger and the hospitals don't have the same kind of systems that we do – it can be a long time before the person's relatives are contacted. But Ehsan had bought several pairs of the same type of sandal and had kept one pair for himself and given the others to Habib, Anwar and Mosen. As a bit of a joke, amongst his friends he was always pointing out how good the dark brown sandals looked on his fair-skinned legs. Soheila was walking by the spot where the accident happened. On the ground, through the legs of the crowd that had gathered, she noticed the same kind of sandal as the one Ehsan had given her husband. She had Ehsan's body taken to the hospital.

The hospital still appears in my nightmares. We went down many flights of steps into the basement. It smelt terrible in the corridor. I followed Mosen into a freezer room where there were probably about fifty or sixty bodies. They must have had no family or friends to come and pick them up because they had been there so long that they had started to dry out. The bodies were in piles all over the floor, stacked on top of each other.

Mosen had agreed to take me to see Ehsan's body only if I promised to keep control of myself. I had said, 'Just show me once and then I will sit quietly,' but now that I saw all the bodies I thought I was going to collapse. Mosen told me to walk slowly, following where he placed his feet, in the spaces between the bodies.

They hadn't put Ehsan on top of a pile of bodies because he was from Australia and he had relatives to look after his body and pay for a funeral. He was lying on a bunk bed. There was a body on the bunk above him, and one on the bunk below. His face was swollen and covered in blood; his body was covered with a sheet.

I said to Ehsan, 'How can you leave me like this? I found a woman for you, and she's beautiful.' Mosen started to get worried because I was talking to a dead man; he covered Ehsan's face with the sheet.

'No, I have to see him again. This is not him.' I pulled the sheet back. 'He's alive, he doesn't look like all these others.' I said a lot of other nonsense – it was as if I'd gone mad.

Mosen said, 'You promised you'd be strong.' He drew the sheet across Ehsan again. I started to black out and he picked me up, put me over his shoulder and carried me out of the room. In the hallway he put me down on the floor and started shouting at me to wake me up. I felt embarrassed then. He took me to the car and drove me home.

~

A few days later Assad and another of his brothers, Shajan, arrived in New Delhi to arrange Ehsan's funeral. I was crazy with grief and barely noticed their arrival. I had stopped talking. If someone dressed me I changed my clothes, otherwise I just kept wearing the same ones from the day before. I couldn't be bothered having a shower. I refused to put on shoes. All I could do was housework: if someone told me to do something I would follow their instructions.

For a couple of days after Ehsan's death Anwar hadn't been able to walk – and even then, when he did start walking again he was very weak. He was worried about me, though, so he made an effort to get better and get out of bed. Assad was in deep shock. He and Ehsan had been so close that people had called them twins.

One of the good things about the Afghani community is that when somebody dies, everyone comes to support the family in their grief. Lots of people came to Ehsan's funeral, and his grave was piled high with flowers. It seemed right for him to be buried in New Delhi because he loved India so much.

Afghanis have a traditional forty-day mourning period. It was planned that at the end of the forty days, Assad and I would be married, but I was obviously in no state for a wedding. I blamed myself for Ehsan's death: the whole reason that he was in New Delhi was to help me and Assad get married. If he hadn't come for that, the accident would never have happened. One day Shajan sat down with me and said, 'It hurts me to see you like this. You are too important to my family. Don't blame yourself – it's not your fault that Ehsan died. God brought him here and God brought him this accident, not you.' He spoke just like Ehsan had. 'He's gone and we have you now. If you want his spirit to be happy and if you want us to be happy, then don't put yourself under so much pressure.'

Gradually, thanks to Shajan's words, I started to recover.

≈

Ever since I was a young girl I had dreamed of having a big
wedding and wearing the white dress and veil that brides
wear in the West. In Afghanistan brides traditionally wear
green but in modern times some change after the religious
part of the ceremony is over into a Western-style bridal
dress and veil for the rest of the wedding party. Because
there had just been a family tragedy there was to be no
party for Assad and me, just a religious ceremony con-
ducted by a sheikh at our home.

The only guests at our wedding would be Khaled, his
mother, sisters and brothers, Habib and Mary, and a few
others. Normally an Afghani wedding party starts around
six or seven in the evening and goes until dawn, with lots of
eating and dancing, but ours would be a simple afternoon
ceremony. I spent the morning cooking food to serve the
guests for lunch. When Khaled's sisters arrived they pulled
me out of the kitchen and told me I had to get ready. I got
into a new green dress, they fixed my hair and green veil up
beautifully, and put a tiny bit of make-up on me. Khaled's
mother was furious when she arrived and saw what they'd
done. She tore the veil off, flattened it down and put it on
me like an ordinary headscarf. She wiped the make-up from
my face. It was too soon after the mourning period for
Ehsan.

In most Afghani weddings the bride and groom sit
together, but in more old-fashioned ceremonies the bride
and groom are separated. I don't know if it was out of

106

respect for Ehsan, but we had the more old-fashioned type. The women, including me, sat in one room while the sheikh performed the ceremony in another room with Assad and the other men. I didn't see the sheikh or Assad. An elder of the community came into the room at one point in the ceremony and asked me if I took Assad to be my husband and I said, 'Yes.'

~

Shajan returned to Australia shortly after our wedding but Assad stayed in India for three months, recovering from his grief and settling into married life. After that I was in India for another three months to finalise my immigration application before I could go to Australia to join him.

For years I had worn the traditional *shalwar kameez* – a loose-fitting outfit that covers the legs and arms and is made up of trousers and a knee-length top. Whenever I went out or men came to visit I wore a scarf to cover my head. Assad asked me to buy some modern dresses for when I arrived in Australia, so I did. To me they were really daring, but of course compared with what women were wearing in Australia they weren't. He also asked me not to cover my head with a scarf when I arrived in Australia.

When I got ready to go to the airport I put on one of the dresses, did my hair – and didn't put on a headscarf. It was difficult for me to walk out of the house like this – and difficult for Anwar too. He said, 'Why don't you at least put your scarf on? I know you. This is not you; you're doing it for him. I don't want to see you changing yourself for someone else.'

I put a scarf on. Anwar took me to the airport and we cried as we said goodbye. He told me that no matter what happened in Australia, he would always support me. If anything went wrong he would come straight away and look after me. It was hard to say goodbye to my brother. I was worried about leaving him alone in New Delhi after all he'd done for me.

As the plane started to move down the runway I took my scarf off, folded it and put it in my bag. I was uncomfortable about having a bare head in front of men I didn't know, but I would do anything Assad asked.

# Chapter 9

The plane had started to descend. My future lay beneath the white clouds out the window: Sydney was down there somewhere. I felt relief and a sense of hope. I may not have actually seen it yet, but I had a home again. I wasn't a refugee any more.

I felt uncertainty, too. I'd heard that Sydney was a big city with tall skyscrapers stretching up into the sky. They were like towers of metal and glass, shiny as mirrors. As the plane neared the airport I got more and more worried – if everything was so new and shiny was I going to be able to walk on the street or would I slip over? Would the pavement be as smooth as glass, too?

Assad, Shajan, his wife, Malia, and a few of their close Afghani friends met me at the airport. Assad and I hugged – he looked so happy to see me. It was winter 1984 and compared to the summer in India it was freezing. Malia gave me a warm jumper to put on. Sitting in Shajan's car being driven through the streets of Sydney I was relieved to see that it wasn't all metal and glass. There were grass and flowers in people's front gardens; there were paved streets and footpaths. I would be able to walk, and get my feet and hands in the soil. I knew everything was going to be okay. I noticed, too, that unlike polluted New Delhi, the air and the streets were clean. On the way to Shajan and Malia's flat in Lane Cove, where we would be staying, they took me to Darling Harbour to see the water. I had seen rivers in Afghanistan, but I had never seen the ocean or a harbour before. I was impressed by its beauty, by how clean and sparkling the water was.

After a few days had passed Assad told me that I would be starting a job that afternoon. I was excited – I'd never had a job before. I had a shower and got dressed in my nicest clothes. Shajan drove Assad and me to a small office block in Artarmon, a couple of suburbs away. When we were inside the building he handed me a big black plastic bag. I'd never seen one like it in my life. I said, 'What do I do with this?' Then I looked around the office and realised it was completely empty. It was five o'clock in the afternoon and everyone had gone home: I was there to clean. Assad explained that Ehsan had been the cleaner at this building before he'd gone to India and now we were going to take his place. We emptied rubbish bins, dusted desks and cleaned toilets until late that night. I needn't have taken a shower beforehand; it was afterwards that I needed one.

After a month we moved into our own place, a one-bedroom flat at Milsons Point overlooking Sydney Harbour. I'd never seen so much water before. The landlord was a generous man who let us rent the place cheaply. We didn't have a very fancy life – we didn't even have a TV for a while – but it felt good to be in Australia, where we were safe and free. Sydney was a beautiful city, the weather was mild – it never snowed and the temperature didn't stay in the high forties all summer long – and the people were friendly and relaxed.

As soon as I came here I felt a part of this country. As soon as I put my feet on Australian land it felt like my home. I loved it straight away, and I loved the people – everyone was kind to me. I didn't experience any racism when I first arrived, and I was amazed at how people from many cultures lived side by side. There was every kind of food, and I saw women wearing headscarves and all sorts of other traditional clothes. Before I came to Australia I had thought that Assad had asked me not to cover my head with a scarf because you were not allowed to wear one here, but now I realised that it was just his preference to be with a more modern-looking woman.

There were lots of things I didn't understand about Australian culture – like how people were always watching what they ate so they didn't put on weight. After years in Peshawar of eating little other than bread and yoghurt it seemed funny to me. Over there everybody wanted to eat, and here everybody was saying: 'Don't eat.' I was thin when I arrived but soon put on some weight. I ate lots of eggs, which I loved but hadn't been able to have for a long time. They tasted different to what I remembered from Afghanistan, and so did the fruit, vegetables, meat and bread. In Afghanistan you didn't have to pay extra for organic, everything was organic.

I felt blessed and lucky to be in Australia, but I would never be able to completely enjoy my new life while I was worried about what was happening to my family on the other side of the world. Immediately I put in an application for Anwar for permanent residency on the grounds of family reunion. I needed a lot of help with filling in the form because I didn't know a word of English when I stepped off the plane. I couldn't apply for my mother and brothers and sisters in Afghanistan because under the Russian regime no emigration was allowed. I still couldn't send letters or ring them in case it got them into trouble. Assad's mother, father, two sisters and brother had recently escaped to Peshawar so he applied for permanent residency visas for them.

I got a second job as a cleaner in a motel during the day. I worked all the time, like a machine, only stopping to sleep and eat. I was driven by the urge to make money – not so that Assad and I could spend it but so that we could send it overseas. We sent most of our spare money back to Assad's family.

At first I used hand gestures and body language to communicate. I took English classes for a few weeks, but after I started the second job I didn't have time. I picked up English by listening to people's conversations on the train and reading magazines. Even though I didn't know many words I wasn't embarrassed about going up and talking to people – I just did the best I could.

~

The first year of my marriage to Assad was a time of hope and new beginnings, but it was also often hard and challenging. Like most refugees it wasn't easy for me to forget the things that had happened in the past or put aside my fears for what might happen to my family. I also battled with loneliness. All my life I'd been surrounded by people – brothers, sisters, cousins, aunts, uncles, visitors. I had barely had a moment alone, now I was in a household of only two people. I wanted us to try and start a family of our own straight away, but Assad said I was still a baby myself and we should wait. He encouraged me to fulfil my dream of getting an education: I could go back to school and on to university, have a career and then start having children. But what I really wanted was to hold a baby in my arms and have a house filled with noise and laughter, like the one I'd grown up in.

Assad was carrying around a lot of sadness. Not only was he separated from his family but he was still grieving. He often looked as though he had the weight of the world on his shoulders. We weren't as carefree as some other couples perhaps are when they first get married, but our relationship was strong. Our flat was on the second floor and I always knew when Assad was coming home because I could hear him running up the stairs. I said, 'Wouldn't it be easier to just walk up the stairs?' He told me that he ran because it meant he would see me a minute earlier.

Whenever I was down Assad tried to help me see the positive side of things, and when Assad was down I gave him all the emotional support that I could. But as time wore on I became worried about him, because it seemed that nothing I said or did could cheer him up or make him forget his worries.

After we'd been at Milsons Point for about a year our landlord said he was moving back to London and needed to sell our flat. He asked whether we would like to buy it. He offered it to us for only $50,000 – a fraction of what it would be worth now – and said we could pay him back gradually. Assad and I didn't want to make that kind of commitment while our family members were still in Afghanistan and Pakistan, so we said no.

Assad decided that what he needed to snap out of his down mood was to try living in a different city. We packed up and moved to Melbourne, even though we knew nothing about it and had no family there. We found a flat in Glen Iris, and I got a job as a machinist in a clothing factory that made men's jumpers. I loved Sydney and didn't want to leave, and I didn't like the weather in Melbourne, but I was hopeful that our move might lift Assad's mood.

Assad got a job in a factory, too. He had to do a lot of lifting there and a few months after we moved to Melbourne he injured one of the discs in his back. He was unable to work and needed a lot of looking after. At first he couldn't do anything – he could barely even pick up a glass to drink from, he was in so much pain. He did lots of exercises to try and fix his back but he still couldn't return to work. It was a difficult time. I had to support us as well as send money back to Assad's family in Peshawar. I remember struggling home on the bus alone with our groceries because we couldn't afford a car.

Around the same time Anwar's application for permanent residency was accepted and he flew to Melbourne and moved in with us. I was full of joy at having my brother by my side again. He got a job in a factory straight away and each month he sent money back to our mother and brothers and sisters in Kabul and gave me some for rent and food. I didn't spend it; I put it in the bank instead.

When Anwar had been in Australia for a year he flew back to be married to Shahla, the girl my father had recommended to him. Before he left I handed him a cheque for a few thousand dollars – the money he had given me for rent and food. He said that I should've spent the money, but it made me feel good to know that I'd made things a little easier for Anwar. I would never be able to pay him back for the sacrifices he had made for me, but at least I could help him get his marriage off to a good start. Shahla joined him in Australia and they got a place together near ours.

I kept reminding Assad how much I wanted a child, and he kept resisting. One afternoon we were walking by the beach at St Kilda, looking out over the water, and I mentioned it again – only this time Assad turned to me, smiled and agreed.

Shortly before I was about to have my first baby, Assad's application for his family's permanent residency was approved. They moved into the flat with us – his mother and father, two sisters, brother and his brother's wife.

In 1986 I gave birth to a beautiful boy with big, dark brown eyes and we named him Arash. When I held him I felt like I had the whole world in my hands. I immediately felt a strong connection with him, a deep understanding. I could sit and talk to him about anything.

I didn't take much time off work after having Arash, asking my in-laws to babysit for me. I wanted to make money so I could provide for little Arash. When I went to work I felt exhausted, though. I couldn't concentrate on what I was doing and I just wanted to go home and rest. After only a couple of weeks I took more leave from work, but I didn't feel any better at home. I found it unbearable to be around people. I had been overjoyed when Assad's family had got their visas and come to live with us but now I found myself resenting them. I wanted to be left alone, and of course that was never going to happen at our flat.

I spoke to Assad about getting a place of our own and he rented us another flat. As the months passed I gradually began to feel and think like my normal self again. My exhaustion and bitter thoughts started to fade. I know now that I was suffering from post-natal depression. Assad was gentle and supportive during this time and several months later when I had recovered I went back to work.

My brother Omar had become engaged to Assad's sister Arozo and he came to Australia to marry her. They moved in with Anwar. Meanwhile, my mother, younger brothers and sisters finally made the journey to Peshawar, with my father, Nadira and their five children. They had left everything behind in Kabul and now all they had was a couple of changes of clothes. They were staying with my father.

I couldn't call them because they didn't have a phone, but at least I could finally write a letter to them. I sat down with a pen and some paper, but I didn't know where to begin. At first I just kept writing over and over how good it was to be able to write to them, because that meant they were safe; the years of anxiety and uncertainty were over.

There were a lot of mouths for my father to feed, and it was especially hard now that he was a refugee. Omar and Anwar sent money so that my mother and younger brothers and sisters could rent their own house. This was a good time for my mother. She could go out shopping, make the household's decisions, and entertain her friends and relatives whenever she felt like it. My brother Assad eventually moved from Tehran to live with my mother, and he got married.

❦

Melbourne didn't live up to Assad's expectations. Moving hadn't made him happy the way he thought it would. He decided we should move back to Sydney. I didn't want to leave Melbourne because it would mean being separated from Anwar and Omar again. But there was nothing I could do to change Assad's mind. We packed up and moved back to Sydney when Arash was one year old and rented a flat in Meadowbank in Sydney's west.

Soon after we moved I became pregnant again. It was 1988, the country was in a recession and jobs were hard to get. I couldn't find work. There were so many people looking for jobs, why would they hire a woman who would soon be leaving to have a baby? Assad was still having trouble with his back and couldn't do the kind of factory jobs he'd done in the past, but he wasn't qualified for other jobs. We were a poor family. There was no money coming in and we were living on social security. We were barely able to cover our rent and bills.

But I gave birth to a lovely baby girl. She was tiny and thin, perhaps because my diet had suffered since our money troubles. When I changed her nappies and her clothes it was like handling a precious little doll. We named her Tamana.

~

I missed my family in Peshawar and I was particularly worried about my sister Zarmina because there were no opportunities for young Afghani refugees in Peshawar. I hoped to bring her to Sydney, where she would have a better chance of a good life. I used my savings to pay for an airfare and I packed my bags and flew to Pakistan, taking Arash and Tamana with me. I knew that I might be in Peshawar for six months or so because I wanted to return with Zarmina and it would take at least that long to apply for a visa for her. We had been finding it hard to afford the rent on our flat in Meadowbank so we had put our furniture in storage and Assad had gone to live with his family, who had moved to Sydney, too.

It was a difficult journey on my own with two tiny children. My brothers Sidiq and Assad met me at the airport. I could hardly recognise them, they had grown up so much. I had flown in to Lahore – about a six-hour drive from Peshawar – because it was cheaper. I was so tired I kept falling asleep on the drive to Peshawar so Sidiq or my brother Assad held Tamana for me.

My mother looked much older, tireder and thinner than when I had last seen her. I could see seven years of worry for her children's safety in the lines on her face. But when we hugged each other it was like nothing had changed – I was back in my mother's arms at last. I didn't want to ever let go.

I didn't recognise my younger brothers and sister at all. They were babies when I left. I said, 'Where is Zargona? I want little Zargona.' She was standing right in front of me, a tall and slender girl in her early teens.

I was shocked when I saw Zarmina. She looked fifty years old, even though she was only in her early twenties. Soon after I arrived in Peshawar I went to the Australian embassy to put in a visa application for her.

It was both strange and familiar to be with my family again. So many things had happened to us that in some ways we had to get to know each other all over again. The stories and emotions that we'd bottled up for the last seven years came flooding out. I cried when they told me of their trip from Kabul to Peshawar. They had gone the same way as me – on foot, on donkey, in buses and squashed into cars. My family and I had shared the same journey. And thousands of other people had taken the same route, or ones that were very similar. My mother, sisters and brothers and I were just little drops that had joined a river of Afghanis pouring out of the country, people whose lives were already so at risk that we didn't mind the additional risk of escaping. We each had our own personal experiences, but on a broader scale we all had the same story to tell.

It was wonderful to introduce Tamana and Arash to their grandmother and aunts and uncles for the first time. They held Arash and Tamana in their arms and smiled and kissed them, something I'd dreamed of seeing ever since my babies were born. Arash got a lot of stomach troubles because he wasn't used to the food in Peshawar, but Tamana was okay because she was feeding from a bottle. She was very happy baby with a smiling face, and brought a lot of joy to the whole family. Everyone loved having her and Arash around.

Within six months Zarmina's application to migrate to Australia was accepted. She and I got ready to leave Peshawar. I longed to be back in Australia again, but it filled me with sadness to leave behind part of my family, especially my mother. I had been in Peshawar for six months, but even that hadn't been long enough for us to share all the stories about the experiences we'd had while we were apart. I could only hope that it wouldn't be another seven years before I saw my mother again.

# Chapter 10

When I returned to Australia we rented a house near Assad's family's, in Penrith in Sydney's west. I got a part-time job working as a cleaner in the mornings. We were still struggling to pay the rent, so six months later when we were allocated a house in Mt Druitt, in western Sydney, by the Department of Housing I was relieved. It would take the pressure off us financially, and I was looking forward to settling down in one house instead of moving around all the time. The best part was that we had a garden and could grow vegetables and flowers. And Arash and Tamana had room to ride bikes and play.

That year, 1989, I became an Australian citizen. It was a good feeling. I was truly a part of the country. I could vote. And I no longer felt the uncertainty of being on a permanent residency visa – they could take away a visa, but they couldn't take away my citizenship. I had a home.

It was good to be settled, but something was bothering me. Ever since I had returned from my trip to Peshawar I had noticed a change in Assad, in the way that he behaved towards me. I didn't feel as though he'd missed me while I was away, and he seemed distant somehow.

I was worried, too, about my mother and brothers and sister in Peshawar. I put in applications for permanent residency visas for them but it was to prove much more difficult for them than it had been for Omar, Anwar and Zarmina. Although I was applying on the same grounds – family reunion – over the next few years their applications would be rejected three times. Each time I appealed the decision I had a tense wait to find out what would happen. It became very depressing; I began to fear I might never be reunited with them. I got help from a solicitor, but he didn't have any success either. Finally, there was a change in government policy and the number of family reunion visas was increased and they were allowed into the country in late 1991. About six months later my brother Assad and his wife and children followed.

~

As they grew up Arash and Tamana became not just brother and sister but the best of friends. They were always together. Tamana was outgoing, friendly and smart. She loved dressing up. Arash had always been a mummy's boy; he liked to be with me all the time. When I went to the toilet he waited outside for me. He washed the dishes with me and talked to me while I cooked. He and Tamana shared their own bedroom but often he liked me to sleep in his bed with him. We were hardly ever separated until he started school.

Like me when I was a child, Arash loved going to school. He was very clever and thoughtful, and was always asking questions. In grade one, at the age of six, his big thing was astronomy. He was always looking up at the night sky asking questions about the stars, the moon and the planets, which I didn't have any answers for.

He thought a lot about God and religion, too. Sometimes I worried whether he thought about it too much. Early one morning as the sun was coming up I heard him scream and then shout out, 'Mum.' I ran into his bedroom and said, 'Arash, what's wrong?'

He said, 'Hold me, hold me tight.' I sat down on the bed and put my arms around him. He was shaking and his skin felt cold.

I rocked him and said, 'You're okay, everything's all right. Did you have a bad dream?'

'No, it wasn't a dream, God called me from the sky. He called my name and his voice was very, very loud and I woke up.'

I said, 'Arash, God's not calling anybody. God doesn't even have a human voice like you and me. You just had a dream.' After a while he stopped shaking and said, 'Okay,' and nodded, but I could tell he wasn't convinced. His behaviour changed from that day. He sat quietly all the time, thinking to himself, 'Why was God calling me?' I have a photo of him that was taken then and even now I can see what he was thinking.

The next morning Arash told me that God had called him again. He said, 'Mummy, how could you stay asleep when the voice of God is so loud?' He begged me to stay awake beside him that night so that I could hear it, too. I was getting worried about him so I spent the night lying next to him in his bed. He slept peacefully all through the night, and when he woke up the next morning he looked at me and said, 'Did you hear it, Mummy?' When I said no he couldn't understand why.

I didn't know what to do. I called Uncle Haji, who had moved to Australia around the same time as me and was living in Sydney. I often turned to him when I had a problem. He wasn't too worried and suggested that I keep doing what I had been doing: reassuring Arash that these were just dreams.

The fourth night I woke up to the sound of Arash screaming and rushed to him. He was shaking even worse than the first time. I said, 'What happened tonight?'

He said, 'I saw God.'

I said, 'What?'

'I saw God. He called my name and said, "Look at me".'

'What did He look like?'

'He was like the sun, bright like the sun. I tried to look right at Him, but it hurt my eyes.'

I was so concerned that I called a sheikh. He said, 'Don't worry, there's nothing wrong with your son. He's going to grow up to be a very godly person. God loves him and has chosen him.' He said that if I wanted the visions to stop I should donate some food or money to needy people and pray to God.

I took his advice, and tried once again to reason with Arash. I said, 'Listen, my son, God is not calling you, you've just been having dreams.'

He said, 'Mummy, you don't know anything. I saw God and He can talk. He calls me all the time.'

I said, 'Well okay, Arash.' I decided to just leave it there and not discuss it any more. I was worried he might be going crazy, and me bringing it up all the time wouldn't help. Besides, the topic of God was too complicated; I couldn't answer his questions. When he talked about God he talked like he was an adult, not a six-year-old.

All that week he asked endless questions about the stars and planets, and about creation. One night he came for a ride with me in the car when I went to buy milk; he spent the whole trip looking up at the sky. I don't think he even heard me when I said, 'Can you come down to the ground? Can you stop thinking about what's up in the sky and look down for a second?'

It was the July school holidays. One of Assad's brothers offered to have Arash or Tamana go and stay with him and his wife and four-year-old daughter in Wollongong for a weekend. They were living in a flat and only had room for one of the children, otherwise we all would have been invited. Arash loved his auntie and uncle and cousin and said he wanted to go. We didn't have any plans to take the kids out so I thought it would be good for Arash to go and have some fun; there are beautiful places to see near Wollongong. I was a bit worried that Arash might get upset being separated from me, especially after all the dreams he'd been having. I said, 'You're not going to cry during the night when you're away?' and he said, 'No, I'm grown up. I'm not a baby.'

They arranged to pick Arash up on Friday and bring him home the following Sunday. On Thursday night I had a dreadful nightmare. Arash had been killed by a car. I was holding his body in my arms, running after the car that had hit him. The dream was so real that when I woke up I had to go to his room to make sure he was okay.

The next day I gave him a shower, dressed him in his nicest clothes and packed his backpack for his trip to Wollongong. We said goodbye and he walked out the front door with his aunt and uncle. He'd only gone a few steps before he turned around, came back and hugged me really tightly. My mother was there and she said, 'Oh Arash, you want to go – but you don't want to go.' I kissed him and said, 'Go on, it's okay.' As soon as I said it I felt like this was the last time I would ever see my son. I had the feeling you get the moment that you drop something, just as it falls from your hand. I talked about Arash all day to my mum – 'Arash did this . . .', 'Arash said that . . .' – because I couldn't stop thinking about him.

On Saturday afternoon I was in the car and heard something on the radio about a tragedy near Kiama, on the coast south of Wollongong. There had been some kind of accident near the blowhole, where people go to watch the sea shoot up through a hole in the rocks. As soon as I heard the word 'Kiama' my heart started pounding. I rushed to my father- and mother-in-law's place, picked up the phone and dialled my brother-in-law in Wollongong. But there was no answer. I let the phone ring and ring, hung up and dialled again. I started to feel panicky.

A few members of the Afghani community arrived at the house, and I asked them what was going on. The women had no idea; the men knew but wouldn't tell me. I paced up and down, and kept dialling the number and listening to the phone ring. More members of the Afghani community arrived. From them I pieced together bits of information: some members of the Afghani community had been swept into the sea at Kiama; Omar had driven down there. I was sick with fear that Arash had been hurt. I was desperate for Omar to come home and tell me if he was in hospital in Wollongong.

After it got dark Omar came home and told us what had happened. My brother- and sister-in-law had gone to Kiama with a group of Afghani people and a huge wave had washed seven of them off some rocks near the blowhole. They had been standing near the water to take a photo.

I said, 'Is Arash alive or dead?'

'I'm sorry, he's dead.'

When he spoke the words it was like he'd lit me with a match. My whole body got hot, and I burned from my head to my toes. I shouted and I screamed and I cried. I couldn't believe it. It was so unreal.

All of my family came to the house, and people from the Afghani community came and went all night, crying and saying prayers. I sat there barely aware of what was going on around me. In the morning I said, 'I want to see my son.' Omar said I wouldn't be able to until the next day, because the doctors had to examine his body.

And then the next morning I said, 'I want to see Arash. I want to hold my son.' No-one wanted to take me because they were scared of how upsetting it would be for me. I said one more time, 'I want to hold my son.' Finally a couple of friends from the Afghani community took me in their car to go and see him. I was like a blind woman, I didn't know what direction I was walking in. They had to hold me up and lead me inside the morgue.

Lying there on a trolley Arash looked taller, older. His eyes were open. He looked up at me just like he was alive. His skin, his face, his arms – he looked the same as the day he'd left to go to Wollongong. I reached out and touched him. I had never touched a dead person before. I didn't know how stiff he would be, like a piece of wood. I thought he would be soft and limp, like in my dream where I held him after the car accident. My friends said, 'Don't you want to hold him?' but I couldn't because his body was so stiff, he was impossible to hold. I sat by his side for a while talking with him and then I left. By the time I got home I was out of control with grief. Then someone gave me a tablet and I slept like I was a dead person.

The next day was the funeral for those who lost their lives at Kiama. I went early in the morning to pray. All

Muslims must be washed by hand in a special ritual before burial, and I went to watch as they washed Arash. He was lying next to his little cousin. After being washed they were wrapped up in white shrouds. They looked like a bride and groom together, so peaceful, so lovely, so clean.

I couldn't believe I was seeing so many bodies laid out in a row. I had thought that once I'd come to Australia I would never see so many bodies lying together, but I guess when it's time to die it doesn't matter where you are. You might die from a bomb, or you might die from going sight-seeing.

I was desperate. I said a silent prayer: 'God is great, God is great, God is great, I can see the power of God, how you can make us live, how you can make us die. God, you have the power to give my son back to me. You were calling him for a week, he saw you in his dream. Now I believe everything my son said. I know you exist, I know God is true, God is great, God has power. Please God, give my son back to me.'

After the funeral service at the mosque we went to Rookwood Cemetery for the burial. There was a row of open graves. Arash's coffin was taken out of a white funeral car and placed by the side of a grave at one end of the row. I wanted to say, 'Please don't put my son at the end, put him in the middle.' I wanted him to have somebody on either side of him. When I tried to speak I couldn't, no sound would come out. I tried to use body language, waving my arms and pointing, but no one could understand me.

And then I saw them take Arash out of his coffin to lower him into his grave. In a Muslim burial the body is laid directly in the earth in its shroud, without a coffin. I tried to say: 'Please leave my son in the box, I don't want you to take him out.' Every night at home I'd tucked Arash into bed, making sure he had enough pillows and blankets. I couldn't bear the thought of him lying in the dirt with nothing to rest his head on and nothing to protect him. I looked like a crazy woman waving my arms and crying, unable to speak. I heard somebody say to one of my cousins, 'It's too much for her, take her home.'

They took me to my in-laws' house. My mother-in-law was there and she hugged me as I cried. She hadn't gone to the funeral or to the cemetery. She grieved differently to me. She didn't cry, shout or scream, or ask God why He had taken so much from her – she prayed quietly. According to Islam everything belongs to God. God gives us life and when He chooses to take life away from one we love we must accept it patiently, as His will. My mother-in-law is a godly woman who truly lives by this. She is an amazing, strong woman.

During the forty-day mourning period, people from the community come and sit with the family of the deceased. They cook and clean for you, pray with you and comfort you. The first three days are considered the most important of the mourning period and you can expect a couple of hundred people to come. Even more people came than usual, including some from the wider Australian community who had learnt about the tragedy in the news. There were so many people that we had to hire a hall in Auburn from the local council. People sat and talked with me but I wasn't even aware. I was in shock. I didn't feel anything. I didn't notice who was coming, who was going. I didn't know whether it was day or night, to me they were the same. It was like a horrible nightmare.

My mother and brothers and sisters were a great help to me. They spent all their time cooking and cleaning and running around getting things done because I couldn't do anything. Even though they were upset and grieving, too, they looked after me and helped out. My mother and younger brothers and sister Zargona had only been in the country for eight months.

Gradually my numbness faded, and then I couldn't stop crying. On the fortieth day of mourning there is one final big gathering of the whole community. And then it's time for everyone to leave you alone with your grief. Once people stop visiting it's just you with your pain and you realise you have to go through it on your own.

# Chapter 11

I realise that in talking about the period after Arash's death I hardly mentioned Assad. Instead of us coming together to support each other we grieved separately. We never really talked to each other about the pain of losing our son. When my mood was blackest and I needed Assad's support he didn't seem able to offer it. I felt as though he had closed his heart to me. Assad was in his own deep state of grief. It was a terrible time for everybody. But it is difficult for a mother to lose a child and then not be able to grieve with her husband. I wanted us to share our pain; I wanted us to comfort and support each other.

After Arash's death we stayed with Assad's family in Auburn. I went back to our house in Mt Druitt only once. The moment I saw Arash's bed I knew I couldn't bear to go in there again. A friend arranged a garage sale and sold most of our things and we went on the Department of Housing's waiting list. Assad, Tamana and I slept on the floor at the two-bedroom flat in Auburn.

My mother-in-law was kind and loving to me. She was strong and dignified in the face of death, but nothing could hide the sadness in her or the rest of the family's faces. The house was a cemetery, everyone talking about dead people all the time, or sitting lost in their thoughts about the dead. I felt it was best for Tamana to get out of the house as much as possible and put her into long daycare from nine o'clock in the morning to six o'clock in the evening so she could play with other kids.

But emotionally Tamana was miserable. She had lost her brother, cousin, aunt and uncle, her home, her clothes and her toys. She was confused. At only three she was too young to be able to fully understand what had happened. She wrote letters to Arash and asked me to post them. Each time I went with her to the post office, put a stamp on the envelope and put it in the mailbox. She was always waiting for a reply. Once she gave a letter to her uncle and asked him to post it in case I was posting the letters wrongly. She cried a lot and had difficulty sleeping. We had to put her in the car and drive around and around until she drifted off. I gave her extra love and attention, because she needed it.

After we spent three months with Assad's family the Department of Housing found us a new house in North Ryde, in Sydney's north-west. It was good to be on our own again because we needed to be in a calm, peaceful place to come to terms with what had happened. But the peace and quiet brought more sadness, because it made it even clearer to me how much Assad and I had grown apart.

My doctor had put me on Prozac shortly after Arash's death, but even so everything looked dark and hopeless to me. I felt darkness in my heart. My vision had actually changed: things looked the way they do when the sun goes behind a cloud, even when there were no clouds in the sky. I hardly slept because every time I lay down and put my head on the pillow I thought of Arash lying in the cold earth. I couldn't get the image out of my head. Tamana started pre-school and I worried about her all the time. I got scared to leave the house in case she was hurt in an accident and I missed the principal's phone call.

After several months like this I woke up one morning and realised there were two ways I could go from here: I could stay at home feeling depressed and alone, sinking deeper into a hole – or I could get out of the house and do something. I thought about what I could do. I didn't want to be a cleaner all my life, but I wasn't trained to do anything else. I decided it was time to go back to school.

I enrolled at Meadowbank TAFE College to do year ten. I had to go right back to the beginning and learn my A, B, C. Most of the other students were people who had grown up in Australia speaking English but for whatever reason hadn't managed to finish high school, or hadn't got the kind of marks they needed to go on to further study. I felt so far behind them and wished that I had learnt English properly when I'd first come to Australia; it would've been easier when I was younger. It was hard to focus on studying because I was still grieving. The teachers knew about what had happened and they were gentle with me. They didn't mind when I left the classroom in the middle of class and stood under a tree far from the school buildings to scream or cry. If I didn't finish an assignment on time they gave me an extension. I made many friends, and I will always be grateful to them for being there for me. They would help me out by looking over my work and giving me their opinion and advice on how I could improve it. Whenever I wasn't looking after Tamana I was studying in the library.

I passed year ten and the next year I enrolled to do a tertiary preparation course. It was like year eleven and year twelve combined into one year for mature-age students who wanted to get into university or college. When I passed all my subjects and graduated I felt like I had really achieved something. I would never be able to become a doctor as I had dreamed of when I was a girl, but at last I had finished school and would be able to do some sort of further study.

The whole time I was at Meadowbank I thought of Arash every moment of the day. The pain was always there. When I was a teenager, before the Russians invaded, the young son of a friend of my mother's died. One day when she was visiting us one of my aunties told her she couldn't imagine how painful it must be to lose a child. The woman said it hurt too much to describe, and that sometimes when she was really upset she could feel smoke coming from her nose, as though there were a fire inside her. I ran into the back yard because I couldn't hold in my laughter. I stood there doubled over, laughing and laughing. Every time I thought about it for the next couple of weeks I burst out laughing. What a ridiculous, lying old woman, I'd thought. One day I was sitting in class and started having trouble seeing clearly. I felt a bit strange so I walked out and went to the tree I always stood under when I needed to cry. Suddenly it felt like there was smoke coming from my nose, as if I were burning inside. And I understood that woman who had lost her son in Kabul.

I visited Arash at the cemetery often. His birthdays and the anniversaries of his death were horrible and nightmar-ish. And I had a lot of headaches and neck pain because I'd stopped resting my head on a pillow at night, hoping that it would prevent me from thinking about Arash lying in the dirt. There was a very caring counsellor at the college who suggested that I try seeing a grief counsellor, so I made an appointment.

The grief counsellor had a nice, calming manner. She got me to lie back in a comfortable chair and relax. She spoke slowly and gently, asking me to close my eyes and think about a box, a beautiful pink box. She told me to put a pillow in the box. I imagined a soft pink pillow and my hands placing it at one end of the box. Then she told me to imagine that Arash's grave had been dug up. 'Now, lie your son in the box and rest his head on the pillow,' she said. 'He's comfortable and peaceful in that box.'

I was distraught when I opened my eyes. I was angry that I had let myself believe this fantasy about pink pillows and pink boxes. Now that the counsellor had made me believe this was the way to make things right, I would have to actually go to Rookwood Cemetery, have Arash's grave dug up and lay him in a nice box with a pillow. I couldn't see how I would be able to rest until I had done it. The grief counsellor apologised and said that this kind of technique usually brought comfort to people.

I never tried grief counselling again. But a breakthrough came one day when I dropped Tamana off at pre-school. Every morning I held myself together until I had said goodbye to her at the door, then when I got back into the car I let myself cry. The teachers knew about our situation and were very kind to me and Tamana. One day when I dropped her off a teacher smiled at me and said, 'Don't worry, Mahboba. Tamana will be okay, she's in good hands.'

I got in the car and thought: 'I'm leaving my daughter, my only daughter, at pre-school for the whole day.' Something clicked in my mind. I closed my eyes and pictured Arash's tiny hand. I imagined holding it and reaching towards the sky and placing it in God's hand. I thought: 'Arash is with God. He is with God, like Tamana is in pre-school,' and that brought me some peace.

I was praying and taking comfort from God more than I ever had in my life. That wasn't the only change. My attitudes and priorities were shifting; I was starting to see the world differently. Arash's death had taught me the value of every human being, how precious each person's life is. I thought about how people can be alive one moment and gone the next, and that once they're gone there's nothing you can do for them, you've lost the chance. You have to show them you care right now. I was beginning to realise how much I loved people.

As these feelings were growing inside me women in the Afghani community started coming to me when they needed someone to share their worries with. I guess that because everyone knew about the sadness I'd experienced they thought I'd understand what they were going through. I found that I loved talking with these women. It made me feel like I wasn't being a victim, that I was helping other people. I realised that this was something worthwhile I could do with my life, but I would need to develop my skills. Now that I had passed my tertiary preparation year there was nothing stopping me. I enrolled at Granville TAFE College to do a certificate in community welfare.

I started to learn how to communicate with people who were having problems in their life, how to find the right help for them from government departments and community organisations, how to help women and children who were being abused. I got a lot of practice at counselling. Someone would role play being a person with a problem and I would have to counsel them; we'd be videotaped and would watch it afterwards to see what we'd done right or wrong. I loved the course because the subjects were practical and I knew that I could put what I'd learnt to use and actually make a difference to people's lives.

I'm not saying that I was a great student – I still struggled a lot with English, and I wasn't good at using a computer.

But I worked really, really hard after hours in the library, handed in all my work on time and managed to keep passing all my subjects.

~

Arash had not learned to swim. The wave was so powerful that he might have been knocked unconscious on the rocks before he even entered the water, but it played on my mind that maybe he could've survived if he'd known how to swim. Shortly after Arash drowned I sent Tamana to swimming lessons. Every time she went off with the teacher into the pool I panicked. It was painful to let her go but I knew I had to: I had to make sure she had the best chance of surviving if she ever fell into the water. I was so relieved each time she came out of the pool alive. It wasn't long before she was swimming like a champion.

I didn't know how to swim. I had never trusted the water, but now I hated it. For about three years after Arash's death even having a shower was difficult for me. I didn't turn the taps on fully but just let a trickle of water come out of the shower because to have a strong jet of water on my face made me think of Arash's last minutes, when he was full of water. Water was my enemy.

I knew this feeling was all wrong and that I had to get over it. What if I was near water and a child fell in and I couldn't do anything to save them? One day when I didn't have any classes I went to the swimming pool at Top Ryde and arranged to have swimming lessons. As a Muslim

woman I can't let any man other than my husband see my
body, so I bought a wetsuit that went all the way down to
my wrists and ankles, and a swimming cap so that my head
would be covered.

I will never forget the moment that I first went into the
water. My teacher was a nice, encouraging young woman.
She stood in the shallow end near the steps and asked me to
follow her down the steps into the water. I felt frozen to the
spot. I told her, 'I will never overcome this fear; I'll never be
able to do it.' She held my hand and said, 'Yes you can, you
can do it.' I said a short prayer, put myself into God's hands,
and started walking down the steps. I thought: 'This is the
time when the water is going to kill me too.' But soon I
realised I was standing waist-deep in the water and nothing
bad had happened to me.

The next week the teacher asked me to put my head
under the water; it was terrifying but I managed to do it.
When she let go of my hand it was a really huge step. I was
on my own. After about three or four lessons I was able to
swim from one side of the shallow end to the other. I felt
good that my fear was gone. I could float on top of the
water; it couldn't harm me.

I found that not only did I feel more positive having got
rid of my fear but I also felt more relaxed and fresher after
I'd been swimming. So many Afghani women were missing
out on this. Back in Afghanistan men sometimes swam in
the rivers but women didn't swim at all.

At college I'd been learning a lot about dealing with
government departments and local councils – it occurred to

me that I might be able to organise swimming classes for other Afghani women. I started making phone calls and found out about a pool in Parramatta that is open only to women on certain days of the week. I approached Parramatta City Council and organised for some funding through their Sport and Recreation program. The council paid for the wages of a swimming instructor. I contacted women in the Afghani community, offering them free lessons.

Twelve women came to learn how to swim. Even though they had never swum before in their lives they didn't have the same fear of the water as I did so they were able to learn quickly. After ten or so lessons they were all swimming in the deep end – I had never graduated from the shallow end. Sometimes I sat by the pool watching and babysitting for the women. I loved to watch them splashing around, enjoying their freedom in the water. I got as much joy out of watching them have fun, laughing and joking with each other, as I would have from swimming myself. Many of them said things to me later like, 'This is the first time in my life I've done something just for me.'

When that group of women had learnt how to swim I organised classes for more Afghani women. All up the classes helped around sixty Afghani women learn how to swim. It became something of a priority in my life to encourage these women to learn and then teach their children so that they could be safe around water. The women ended up not just teaching their children but other Afghani women as well. And after the lessons were over, whether I went with them or not the women kept on swimming.

One of the other benefits of the swimming lessons was that it got the women thinking about their health and fitness, often for the first time in their lives. Seeing how successful the swimming classes had been I approached an organisation called Women Speak Out and they gave me funding for exercise classes for Afghani women. They paid for a room in one of Parramatta Council's buildings and a fitness instructor to teach aerobics and stretching exercises to music. Some of the women who had come to the swimming classes came, plus some new women from the Afghani community. I called them all individually to encourage them to come. I joined in the classes, too. It was the first time I or the other women had done anything like this; in the Afghanistan that we had escaped from the only exercise we ever did was at school. We found the classes difficult but really enjoyed them. By the end of the eight-week course we looked fitter and felt happier.

I began to think about how Afghani women had been taught hardly anything about looking after their health. I got involved in the Health Department's Healthy Woman program, which involved having a teacher come out once a week for a few weeks to tell the women how to do things like check their breasts for breast cancer, or have regular Pap smears, or watch their diet to prevent heart disease and osteoporosis. I rang around the women I already knew from the swimming and exercise classes and got together a group of about twenty women who came to listen to the talks each week. Until I'd started going to college I had never known about checking my breasts and things like that, so I knew the other women wouldn't know either. When the teacher told them how important it was to look after their health, and how serious it could be if they didn't, they really focused and took it in.

Most of these women had led disadvantaged lives. They had been through the trauma of war in Afghanistan; they had seen their families killed by bombs or bullets or murdered as political prisoners; they had faced incredible danger escaping their country. And most had grown up thinking that as women they should not have high expectations about what they could do with their lives. I wanted them to be active and outgoing and to have more of a say in their future. I wanted them to make the most of the opportunities that their new lives offered them.

Without good English skills these women would always struggle to succeed in Australia. I approached my college, Granville TAFE, to fund English classes for the women. I knew that a short course wasn't going to be enough – I asked for them to fund a long-term program of weekly classes. The college agreed, paying for a classroom for us once a week at the Migrant Resource Centre in Parramatta, and a teacher.

I gave information about the English course to SBS radio and an announcer read it out during the Afghani program, and I called the women I already knew from the swimming and exercise classes. I didn't put an age limit on the classes – anyone could come – but some of the older Afghani women said, 'It's no use, we'll never be able to learn.' I encouraged them to give it a try and told them that it was possible, it would just mean giving their time and energy. Eventually I got about thirty women to enrol in the classes.

The women weren't used to going to school and some of them faced family pressures, so at first they needed a lot of support. I had to call them and encourage them to come and sometimes I needed to go and pick them up and bring them to class. But once they got into the routine and saw how friendly the classes were they didn't need any encouragement. At first they might have been a bit unsure of what the classroom environment would be like because their education had been disrupted when they were girls. Then they realised they could come each week and be with a group of women who all spoke their language and were all facing the same difficulties learning English and settling in to Australia. They brought along Afghani cardamom tea and their own homemade sweets, and after class they sat and chatted. The teacher won their trust straight away – she wasn't Afghani but she was a Muslim and understood their culture and religion, as well as how hard it was for them to return to study as adults. The women were on their way to a whole new way of life in Australia.

~

Since the day of Arash's funeral I had never stopped asking God to give me my son back. My prayer hadn't brought Arash back when his body was laid out before me at the mosque, but I felt that God could bring him back to me by giving me a new son. I longed to have another baby, a baby boy just like Arash.

The shock of Arash's death, and my ongoing grief, had affected my hormones. A year or so into my community welfare course I went to the doctor and he prescribed some medication to get me back to normal.

Physically, I was ready to get pregnant, but Assad and I hadn't managed to break down the wall that had grown between us since Arash's death. Assad wasn't certain if having another child was the right thing to do given the trouble we'd been having together.

After a couple of months I started developing side effects from the medication – hot flushes, headaches, nausea – and the doctor said I could only take it for one more month. I finished the tablets, hoping Assad and I would reconcile, but on the last day Assad and I were as far apart as ever. I stayed awake until two in the morning, crying and praying.

That night while I was praying I felt a strong connection with God like I have never felt before. The next morning I felt incredibly calm and peaceful. I wasn't upset with Assad; I was patient. This new mood lasted throughout the week and then Assad surprised me by asking if I wanted to go and see a movie and have dinner. It was the first time we'd had a night out together for years. It was like things were back to normal.

The doctor didn't think it was possible for me to fall pregnant but I had stopped worrying about it ever since my night of praying – I understood that it was in God's hands.

After some time had passed I knew in my heart that I was pregnant. I went to the doctor and told him. He laughed and said, 'I've been a doctor a long time. You couldn't be pregnant. You're just convincing yourself you are.'

I left his surgery and went to a nearby medical centre. The doctor gave me a pregnancy test and said, 'The result is positive.' I knew what he'd said, but I asked him to tell me again. He said, 'The result is positive, you're pregnant.' My prayers had been answered.

I had bad morning sickness. One day at about four months pregnant I was at my mum's house and had been vomiting so much that I'd become weak and shaky. I lay down, fell asleep and dreamt the most beautiful dream I have ever had.

An angel with big wings was flying towards me. As he got closer I recognised him: it was Arash. He said to me, 'I am in your belly. Look up into the sky, I'll show you.' Up in the sky I could see my pregnant belly. There was a door in it. Arash the angel opened the door and I could see my baby curled inside me. And the baby was Arash. He was wearing the same clothes he'd been wearing when he drowned. Arash the angel said, 'I'm waiting here to come back. You have to be patient.'

When I went for my ultrasound I told them I didn't want to know the sex of my baby. If they told me it wasn't a boy I would get upset, and that might harm the baby. I loved girls just as much as boys and would have cherished another daughter, but my dream had raised my hopes that Arash was returning to me. I longed desperately to see his face again.

I had a long labour. The contractions would start getting closer together but then they'd stall at the same rate for hours and hours. The longer it dragged on the more unbearable the pain became. I had gone into hospital in the morning and in the afternoon the doctor told me I would not be giving birth that night, but I might the next day. I said to myself, 'It can't go on that long, I don't have that much energy.' I remembered someone telling me that a drink made with warm water, sugar and ginger would speed up a woman's labour, so I mixed some up and had quite a few glasses. My contractions started coming closer together and by about nine o'clock that night I was ready to give birth.

Zarmina was with me in the delivery room. The rest of my family was at home, waiting. I was excited but also scared to see whether the baby was a boy or a girl so I asked the nurses and doctor not to tell me straight away, to leave it to Zarmina to tell me when I was feeling ready. When the baby arrived one of the nurses was so thrilled she burst out, 'It's a little boy!' I couldn't quite believe her. I needed to hear it from my sister's lips. I asked Zarmina, 'Is it a boy?' She was crying. She nodded and said, 'Yes, Mahboba, it's a boy.'

I cried when they put him on my chest and I looked at him for the first time. 'That's Arash, that's really him,' I thought. He had the same eyes, the same skin, the same nose, the same hair. When Assad came to the hospital and looked at our new son he was shocked. He said, 'He looks exactly how Arash did when he was born.' We called him Sourosh.

After I gave birth I was exhausted but I wouldn't close my eyes; I had to watch over my baby. The nurse said, 'Why are you doing this to yourself? Go to sleep and we'll look after your baby in the nursery.' But I'd seen the nursery: there were so many babies there, how could they be sure they wouldn't mix my baby up with another little boy? I had only just got my son back; I wasn't going to take any risks. She made up an identification tag for him, got me to check it was correct, then put it around his wrist. It wasn't enough for me. I didn't let her take him to the nursery but kept him right beside me.

Once I had taken Sourosh home I realised that I couldn't be overprotective of him any more, for his sake. And I knew I had to be careful not to give him special treatment, because he and Tamana were equally precious to me. Tamana was happy because she had a brother again.

Forty days after Sourosh's birth we had a big party, as is the Afghani tradition. It was a really wonderful time for our families, and the whole Afghani community. They'd been there through the tragedy and now they were there to celebrate and share in the good times.

When Sourosh was a few weeks old I went back to finish the last semester of my community welfare course. I took him with me to class; luckily he was a fairly quiet baby.

It would be several years before I fully understood that Arash was gone, because Sourosh looked almost identical to him until he was about three. The two of them even had similar personalities, gestures and facial expressions. But of course Sourosh developed his own character as he got older. I gradually came to accept that I had lost Arash, and that Sourosh is his own person. That doesn't make him any less of a miracle to me.

# Chapter 12

Six months after I had given birth to Sourosh, Assad came to me and said he didn't think we had a marriage left and that he couldn't live with me any more. Even though it was obvious things weren't good between us I was shocked by his words. I didn't know what to do. We were in the midst of a mourning period for two of his relatives who had recently died. I asked him to wait until the fortieth day of mourning; I would help out with the cooking for the final big gathering of the community and then I could think about it more clearly.

When the mourning period ended I told Assad that I would take Tamana and Sourosh and spend a couple of weeks with my father, who was living in Brisbane. After marrying against my father's wishes in India we hadn't been close, but when Arash died he had rung to offer his sympathy. We had been speaking to each other regularly on the phone since then, and I had been to visit him in Brisbane.

I told Assad, 'If you find it's better with me gone, then we can divorce. But if you decide you want me back, call me and I'll come back.'

I didn't feel as brave as my words sounded. If Assad decided he was better off without me I would be devastated. He was the first man in my life. And I'd been brought up to believe that divorce was disastrous for a woman. When I was a girl in Afghanistan divorce wasn't even something that entered a woman's mind. Whether you would have a good life or bad life depended on luck. You had to accept your husband – if he was good, if he was bad, if he hurt you, or if he loved you. If you got divorced you could expect to lose the support of your family or community, and you would be forever labelled as a bad woman.

I spent a couple of anxious weeks with my father, then Assad called and asked me whether I would come home. I returned to him with the children straight away. We lived together for a couple of months but things didn't improve for us. This time Assad went away – he went to Perth for a few weeks to visit one of my cousins who is a good friend of his.

The morning after he left for Perth I woke up feeling tired and miserable. Later that day someone said, 'Mahboba, what's happened to your hair?' I felt the top of my head: there was a bald patch. My hair must have been thinning for some time but overnight so much had fallen out that it had become noticeable. Eventually I went to the doctor, who told me that my hair had probably fallen out due to stress. It grew back after about four months.

I wasn't particularly concerned about losing my hair; I was actually happy about it because now at least I had a good excuse to wear a headscarf when I went out, something that Assad still didn't like me doing because it seemed old-fashioned.

When he returned from Perth I tried hard to capture his heart again, but we had drifted too far apart; we hardly spoke. I lay awake at night feeling sad about what had become of our marriage. Sometimes when I looked over at Assad sleeping, covered with a blanket, I just cried and cried and cried.

After nearly a year of living this way Assad suggested that we try a separation. He took a few of his things, said goodbye and moved out. I felt destroyed. In my eyes I had lost everything. The last thirteen years were a waste; all the effort I'd made was for nothing. Everything I'd worked hard for was gone. It was as if it had all been washed away.

And suddenly I was faced with the difficulties of being a single mother. I found myself having to be not just a mother but a father, too, and it was a huge responsibility. As a single mother you have to do everything for your children: there's no-one else to help you out when it's the middle of the night and your baby is crying for milk and you've run out; to help you when your kids are sick; to drive them to school or to sport; to go to parent–teacher night or the school play.

Even though Assad had not been working due to his back injury, now that he was gone I worried about providing food, clothing and housing for the children on my own. I went on the single mother's benefit. Fortunately I didn't have to pay a lot of rent to the Department of Housing. I tried to make sure that Tamana and Sourosh had everything they wanted. I lived – and still live – a simple life so that I could buy them what they needed. I hardly ever buy clothes or shoes or anything else for myself. I borrow things from my sisters, and sometimes I borrow money from my family to pay for things for the children. But I never discuss financial hardship with them – I don't want them worrying about that.

Emotionally the children were disturbed. Every evening when it started to get dark and Sourosh realised that Assad wasn't coming home, he cried for about an hour, calling out for his father. His swimming teacher arranged a night for all the children's fathers to come and watch the lesson. I asked my mother to come along and watch instead. He was happy that his grandmother was watching him, but it was not the same as having his father there. When Assad came to pick the kids up to spend a day with them Sourosh was always trying to think up ways to get him to come inside the house, asking him to replace a light bulb or look at one of his new toys. I remember being at a shopping centre once and Sourosh saw a family sitting and eating together in the food court and he said, 'I wish I had a family to sit and eat with.' It made Sourosh sad to see his uncles playing with their children – he wanted that, too. I knew how he felt: when

156

I was out in public and saw couples who were happy it made me feel even more lonely.

Tamana became withdrawn and quiet. Only now is it becoming clear just how devastating it was for her to have the family split up. Recently she told me that someone once asked her to name the worst thing that had happened in her life, and she'd answered that it was her mother and father breaking up. She had already been through a lot of grief.

Tamana and Sourosh's supply of love had been halved so I tried to double my love to make up for it. It is painful to go through a marriage break-up, but seeing what it has done to your children is what brings you the most pain.

I felt completely responsible for Tamana's and Sourosh's futures now, so I put a new focus on their education. I started saving so I could eventually pay for private schooling and after-school tutoring, because education will enable them to create good futures for themselves. I worried about them because the job of protecting them was mine alone now. I realised that I needed to talk openly with them about all the issues they would face as they grew up.

Our house was broken into several times after Assad left. I felt vulnerable being alone, and this just made it worse. I'd get home and find the front door open, and would make the children stay in the car while I went inside. I was so scared going in alone, heading straight for the phone in case someone was still inside. Our things would be turned out all over the floor. The thieves got some of my and Tamana's jewellery and a little bit of my money. I no longer felt secure at night and I worried that on my own I wouldn't be able to protect the children should someone break in to hurt them. The kids and I would get really scared when we heard strange noises outside in the darkness. One night I called the police because we were woken by heavy footsteps on the roof. I screamed down the phone that the footsteps were coming closer to the door and the man would be inside the house any minute. The police came and looked up on the roof. They found a possum. Finally I installed security alarms and have never been broken into since.

I encouraged Tamana and Sourosh to see Assad and his side of the family because it was important that they maintain these relationships. I had always believed that I too had a close bond with Assad's family. To me we were like links in a strong chain that could never be broken. So it was a big shock to me that after Assad left they no longer came to visit as they had before, even though they lived only a few streets away. I would see them at the shops and they would walk away as though they hadn't seen me. I still ask myself why our relationship ended – I don't believe that I ever hurt them.

In front of Tamana and Sourosh I acted like everything was okay. It was when they went to bed that I did my crying. For a while I didn't even see much of my family; I didn't want to make them go through any more suffering. Some nights the kids would sleep over at Assad's but instead of using this as an opportunity to go and see my family I would hide from them and spend the night at home, crying and letting out all the emotions I had been trying to hide from the children.

At night on my own I was alone with my thoughts. I couldn't switch off my mind. I stayed awake asking myself why I wasn't successful in my marriage. What was wrong with me? I went over and over everything in my head: all the nice things I'd done for Assad, all the grief we'd gone through, all the stress we'd put our families through when we got married. I thought about little things, like how every day I'd slice fresh fruit and bring it to him on a plate, just to be nice. And for what? The more I thought about everything the more bitter I got.

The worst thing was that I couldn't switch off my feelings for Assad. I had spent so long with him that our relationship was a part of me. I swung from one day remembering only the hurt and pain to other days remembering only the good things about our marriage and desperately wanting him back, even if only for the sake of Tamana and Sourosh.

Omar had moved to Perth with his wife, Assad's sister, Arozo. He came to see me at home one night when he was visiting Sydney. He knew I was very upset and asked me to tell him what was going through my mind.

'I don't want to be a divorced woman. I can't let go. I really want me and Assad to get back together,' I said.

He told me that it was like I had a poison arrow stuck in my heart. 'The moment you pull this arrow out and throw it away your heart will start to heal,' he said. He told me that I'd learn to live with the scar, which would be covered by new experiences and new people in my life, just like the ground becomes covered by leaves falling from a tree.

'There are two things you can do now. You can keep thinking about Assad and be a victim and let this break-up destroy your life – eventually you'll get depression and you won't be able to look after your children, and you'll die slowly, just passing your time. Or you can take all of this pain and turn it into strength,' he said.

I told him I didn't feel strong.

'Turn your pain into power and strength. You can say, "I don't want to be a victim. I'm a fighter," and get on with your life. Put the past behind you and go forward. You'll see, you'll come out of this. You've done it before, you can do it again. There's nothing I or anyone else can do for you this time. Only you can do it for yourself.'

When Omar said goodbye to me at the door I held back my tears because I didn't want him to see how upset I was. He left and I closed the door. A minute or two later when I looked out the window I saw him standing under the tree in my front yard with his back to me. He was crying.

Omar's advice always had a great impact on me and my brothers and sisters. His words to me that night were written on my mind as clearly as if they had been printed in a book in front of me. Later, I thought, 'He's right. Why should I be a victim? I have to be a fighter. I always was a fighter and I always will be a fighter.' It was time to stop agonising over Assad. I would go out and get as much help and advice as I could, and I would start to rebuild my life.

I knocked on many doors. Whatever help I could get, I

took. I saw a counsellor. She gave me a bath towel and said, 'Close your eyes and imagine Assad sitting in front of you and say what you want to say to him. Say it loud; cry, shout, scream if you like. Wring the towel hard.' And then she went off to sit somewhere and watch me.

I started doing what she asked but I felt silly. I thought, 'What an idiot I am, paying $120 an hour to do this nonsense.' I only went a couple of times and then I said to her, 'I'm sorry, your technique isn't working for me.'

This experience, added to my earlier one with the woman who had asked me to imagine giving Arash a pillow and a box, made me realise that counselling was never going to work for me unless I found someone who understood the culture I'd been brought up in.

When you're truly searching for something it will come to you. Someone told me about a class for Afghani women held each Sunday at a woman's home in Auburn, so I went along. There were about twenty women there. The teacher was Mariam, a tall, thin woman in her mid-thirties. She wore a long, flowing dress and was very modestly covered with a shawl; she reminded me of pictures of the Virgin Mary. She was softly spoken, polite and, I realised when she started speaking to the class, well educated and widely read. The class was about how to be a good wife, mother and friend according to Islam. She taught us how to connect ourselves with God, and she asked us to practise the acceptance of others.

Straight away I thought Mariam was lovely and that her teachings were something I needed to hear. I started going to her class every Sunday. The class had to move from her house to the local mosque because it got too big.

Mariam taught Afghani women how to stand on their own two feet. She spoke about women's rights in Islam. What she said surprised me because I had never studied religion properly before: I hadn't realised all the rights that women have under Islamic scripture. Many of the rules that discriminated against women in Afghanistan had no basis in religion but were traditions and customs that had been passed down to us throughout history.

Mariam and I became close friends. We visited each other often and spent many hours together. I talked to her about my marriage break-up, and when I was upset and crying she comforted me and talked me through it. One day I got really upset when I heard about a picnic that Assad was going to. I couldn't bear the thought that after thirteen years of marriage he was out enjoying himself without me. Mariam listened patiently and then she said, 'Mahboba, you talk about Assad all the time. He is a human being, not God. Next time, when you think about Assad, what about trying to switch your mind from him to God?' It was the best advice I got. Whenever I found myself thinking about Assad I swapped him with God in my mind, and the pain of my marriage break-up faded away.

Mariam also helped me to finally stop dwelling on how Arash was lying in the dirt without a box or a pillow. She explained to me that people come from the dust and go back to the dust, so it is natural for our bodies to be in contact with the dust when we die. The part that mattered,

Arash's soul, had gone to heaven. I understood – not just in my head like before but now in my heart – where my son's soul was. I could let my fear and worry go.

Once again I began to cover my head with a scarf whenever I left the house. I started trying to make myself a better person. For my body I went to the gym and got fit; for my soul I read religious books, and went to Mariam's classes and other lectures about Islam. I took comfort in praying. Every night while the kids were asleep I got down on my prayer mat and talked to God. I talked to Him about what had happened in my marriage. I asked Him to help me understand where it had gone wrong. Other times I asked Him to help me understand myself. Some nights I just sat down and closed my eyes and said nothing. Other nights all I could do was cry and say God's name.

After a while I could see an improvement. It looked like this was the medicine for me. When Arash died I just went ahead and took the medication the doctor gave me, but after my marriage break-up I didn't take any pills; I got better by talking with God. I was alone at night and had no-one to talk to – but I could talk to God and He would listen to me and understand me. On my prayer mat I could reveal everything about myself, whether good or bad. Some nights I could feel a beautiful energy come to me; this energy filled my whole body, from my head right down to my toes. After a couple of hours' praying, I felt in charge again and knew I would be able to cope with whatever difficulties there might be the next day. I found that my life was getting better and I had more energy and could do much more than I ever had before.

At night I also spent time practising something that Mariam had taught me: I would think back over what had happened during the day and if I had said or done something that might be hurtful to someone else I asked God for forgiveness. By the end of the day I'd always made a few mistakes, but in the past I had been too busy to stop and reflect. I just went to sleep at night and got up the next day, and maybe made the same mistakes again. I hadn't dealt with the mistakes I'd made and over the years they'd added up.

So each night I closed my eyes and imagined that any hurtful thing I might have said that day was like a black spot on my heart that I needed to clean away. I asked God for forgiveness and made a promise to myself that I would try not to say the same thing again. The mistakes I cleansed myself of were the kind of things most of us do every day to make life easier, such as telling little white lies. Like once when I was on the couch, exhausted, in the middle of watching a movie and someone rang. I knew they were going to be on the phone for a long time so I pretended I was just about to go out. That night I questioned why I'd lied rather than telling the truth: that I was tired, needed a rest and couldn't talk right now.

After many months of praying and cleansing my heart, I started to notice that whenever I was about to do or say something wrong – even though it might only be a tiny little thing – there was a strong voice inside me telling me to think twice. When your house is really clean, if you see some mess you go and clean it up straight away, but if the house is dirty, who cares, you just leave it there. I think that our hearts are the same. But I'm not saying I stopped making mistakes; I do make mistakes every day, just like everyone else.

The second part of the exercise was that when someone said or did something hurtful to me, that night I would practise forgiving them in my heart, and then I would pray for them. It made me feel better to create love instead of hate. Hate hurts you more than the person you hate; and creating a feeling of love creates peace and love within yourself. I started to learn not to judge people.

I followed another of Mariam's suggestions: I wrote a list of the good parts of my personality and the parts that I wasn't so proud of. I stuck the list on the fridge door and started trying to change the things I didn't like about myself, one by one. I started at the top of the list and spent a few months on the first one, concentrating really hard on being its opposite. When I felt I'd made some improvement I moved on to the next point on the list, spent a few months on that, and kept on going until I had reached the bottom.

When I had done things for people I got upset if they didn't thank me or do something for me in return. My expectations had been too high and when people hadn't met them I'd got upset – like when I drove myself mad thinking about all the nice things I'd done for Assad when we were married. So for a few months I practised helping people and not expecting anything in return. If people thanked me or did something for me that was great. If they didn't, I didn't let it worry me. I felt that I should be able to give myself to people just because I love people. And as soon as I started to do things for people without expecting anything from them I felt much happier.

I used to get too easily upset when things didn't go my way. Whenever Assad and I had disagreed about something I'd stayed upset all day, or when someone had said something about me that I didn't think was very nice I'd felt incredibly hurt for a long time. I practised trying to let things go rather than staying angry about them for hours or days afterwards. I was hurting only myself by staying angry.

I had made myself physically sick in the past as a result of seeking attention. With Assad, if I didn't feel like I was getting enough attention from him I found myself saying things like, 'I have a headache,' or 'I don't feel good, I've got a stomach-ache.' Gradually I would start to feel sick, or get a headache. I had such bad headaches that sometimes I wasn't able to open my eyes. I had just been seeking attention at the beginning but then I was truly in pain. I saw doctors, who prescribed medication for the pain. Now I questioned why I had brought these physical pains on myself – and the answer was that I needed attention and love that it wasn't possible to get in my marriage. I kept clinging to our marriage even though our relationship had broken down. By working through this point on my list I came to realise how emotionally sick I had been.

There were many other things on the list but the hardest one of all was that I had lied to myself. Even as my relationship was breaking down I had pretended to myself that I was happy in my marriage. Learning not to lie to other people is hard. It's not easy to be truthful when you're at home and don't feel up to talking to someone but learning not to lie to yourself is the hardest thing of all.

No-one wants to go through a marriage break-up, but I learnt a lot about myself after Assad left. I came to understand why I am in this universe: to try and help others. And understanding why you're here is the start of finding your power and strength. It is a really good feeling to know what you want to achieve from life. I learned that Omar was right: you can take the pain and the sadness in your life and turn it into strength, and you can survive by choosing not to be a victim.

When Assad left, the first thing that came into my mind was that my life was destroyed. The world looked so dark without him. I wish that somebody who had experienced a marriage break-up before had told me: 'Mahboba, your life is not dark. The future is bright.' Day by day I healed and found a little more peace, and eventually the light started to return to my life. I feel sorry for the many women living in Afghanistan who have lots of pressure or even abuse from their husbands and can't switch on that light for themselves. I've made a promise to myself that I am not going to spend even one more hour of my life being upset because of a man. No man on this planet can make me unhappy; I won't let him. I want to be happy.

The final thing I learned in the time of reflection after Assad and I separated is that you don't need to go to university to understand yourself. Life itself will bring the understanding to you if you search for it. It might take a few years of hard work, but it's better to do a bit of work than die never having understood yourself.

~

The Afghani women's English class was continuing into its second year. It was a joy to see how good the women were becoming at speaking English, and how confident that was making them in other parts of their lives. Several of the younger women had moved on to study other courses at Granville TAFE College. Going to the class each week took my mind off my problems, at least for an hour or two.

It felt good to be helping other Afghani Australian women who'd lived through the kinds of things I had, or worse. But I felt worried about the ones who weren't as lucky as us: those who were still in Afghanistan, or living in crowded refugee camps in Pakistan and Iran. The end of the Russian occupation in 1989 had not solved their problems. The Soviet Union had continued to support the communist government in Afghanistan with economic aid. When the Soviet Union broke apart in 1992 the Afghan Government fell. Seven Mujaheddin groups joined together to set up a new government. They became known as the Northern Alliance, but they came from many tribal and ethnic groups and there was so much disunity between them that soon there was a civil war. Law and order broke down outside Kabul and rival Mujaheddin warlords fought each other for control of different regions of Afghanistan.

In 1994, a new group of fighters formed and started taking control of parts of Afghanistan: the Taliban. By 1995, when I was doing my community welfare course, the Taliban were in control of the south and western parts of Afghanistan and were moving to take Kabul. Rocket attacks and fighting amongst Taliban and rival Mujaheddin groups killed many people in Kabul and destroyed the city's buildings. Fighting in the rest of the country left thousands of others dead. The economy was ruined and people were starving. They were leaving their homes and fleeing to other parts of Afghanistan or to refugee camps across the borders.

I only knew what was going on from Afghani refugees who had fled the country. It never made it onto the TV and hardly ever into the newspaper; you didn't hear anyone talking about it on the news. There was a disaster unfolding in Afghanistan and it seemed like the rest of the world hadn't noticed.

During a break at the Afghani women's English class one day a friend of mine, Laila, dropped in to show me a letter that she had just received from a friend of hers in Peshawar, a young woman doctor named Nasrin Nadree. Laila had studied with her in Peshawar, and Dr Nasrin was now working in a hospital for Afghani refugees near the Jalozai refugee camp. The letter had affected Laila strongly and she needed to share it with someone.

I unfolded it and began to read. It was a desperate plea. Dr Nasrin wrote of homeless refugees living on the footpath out the front of her house. She had passed dead orphan refugee children on her way to the bus stop to go to work. Children were dying from starvation and sickness. Sometimes they had to eat grass to try and stay alive. She wrote: 'Can somebody help us, please? Help these children, please.'

I started crying. I stood up and read the letter to the class, and the other women started crying. We sat and cried for several minutes, thinking about the children. They'd known nothing but war. Thousands had been killed in the fighting, and many more had had one or both parents killed. There were thousands of kids with no homes, food, clean water, clothing or schools.

Suddenly it was like a switch went on in my mind. I thought: 'How long should I cry for these children who are dying? What good is sitting here crying going to do?' I said to the other women: 'Stop crying. Let's do something. Let's put together whatever money we can spare and send it to Dr Nasrin.' Still standing out the front of the class, I stretched my hands out in front of me. The women came up and put money in my hands. I counted it up: it came to $120. I gave the money to Laila to send to Dr Nasrin.

A while later I received a letter from Dr Nasrin thanking me and the women in the class. She had distributed the money to thirty-five orphaned children. With her letter Dr Nasrin included a piece of paper with the thumbprints of the thirty-five children on it. Most people in Afghanistan are illiterate so giving a thumbprint is the same as signing your name. It was their way of confirming that they had received the money we sent to Dr Nasrin. One of the orphans who could write had written a message: 'Thank you, Mother. Thank you. We had no hope that anyone would help us. Thank you for giving us hope.'

On that day my life changed. I became the mother of thirty-five orphans. Seeing their tiny thumbprints I knew I couldn't turn my back on them. I thought about Tamana and Sourosh and how lucky they were to have been born in Australia, to have always had a house to live in, a school to go to, food to eat, and to never have had to worry about war. And I thought about Arash – I knew how terrible it was to lose a child. I could not let these orphans die. I would do everything I could to make sure they had some-where to live, food, medical care, and maybe one day an education.

I didn't know anything about fundraising. But I had some Afghani jewellery and bedspreads that I could sell. The jewellery was mostly earrings and pendants made from sterling silver in traditional Afghani designs. The bedspreads were handmade and heavily decorated with gold thread.

One weekend I took some of the jewellery and bed-spreads and went to Merrylands Park, near Parramatta, where there were a lot of Afghani families. I walked up to Afghani people and asked them if they would buy them; I told them that the money would go to help refugee orphans in Pakistan. A few people I approached were interested and bought things from me. Other weekends I went to different parks in western Sydney where Afghani families gathered, and sold more. When the women in Mariam's Sunday class heard about what I was doing they started bringing their bedspreads to me to sell.

I kept a white china casserole dish on top of one of my kitchen cupboards – I still have it – and every day I dropped two dollars of my own money into it, as well as the money I made from selling things to the Afghani community. At night I dreamt about the orphans and how much they needed my help. I asked myself how I was going to raise enough money to give them a good life. Then it occurred to me: moneyboxes. I went to a discount shop and bought twenty money boxes for a dollar each. I gave people in the Afghani community and women in Mariam's Sunday class moneyboxes for their families to place donations in. At the end of the month they gave their moneyboxes to me to be emptied. The first time, I took the money to the bank but they wouldn't accept it because there were so many different types of coins mixed up together. So each month Tamana and I counted them all out in piles: five-cent, ten-cent, twenty-cent pieces, and so on. I did babysitting at night to increase the amount I could send to Dr Nasrin. Each month I would send her whatever I had raised.

Some people didn't trust me when I asked them to make a donation or buy something, because they didn't know me and didn't know what I was doing with the money. I got Dr Nasrin to send photos of the orphans, and each month after I sent the money Dr Nasrin would send fresh fingerprints from the children acknowledging that they got the money, so I showed the photos and finger-prints to people as proof. Gradually everyone started to trust me.

I knew nothing about accounting, but I worked out my own system of recording all the money I received and sent to Dr Nasrin in a notebook. I kept records of the finger-prints I received from the children. I didn't have an office or a filing cabinet – my dining table was covered in sheets of fingerprints, photos and letters; my loungeroom floor was covered in piles of coins.

I had met a wonderful woman named Margaret whose son went to the same pre-school as Sourosh. We would chat when we dropped off or picked up the kids and one day I invited her to have a picnic at Ryde Park. I mentioned the fundraising I was doing and that night she had a dream that she should help me raise money for the orphans in Peshawar. A good friend I had made when I was at Meadow-bank TAFE College, Tania, also started helping me out. They were my first Aussie volunteers.

I began to develop a good working relationship with Dr Nasrin. At first we sent letters back and forth but eventually we started calling each other on the phone to talk about the needs of the orphans. I usually managed to send about two hundred dollars a month to Dr Nasrin, and she gave it to the orphans in a mixture of cash, food and medicine.

I became less closely involved in the English classes I had organised for Sydney Afghani women, handing over my responsibilities to Granville TAFE College. I raised money day and night; the orphans in Peshawar had become the focus of my life.

# Chapter 13

Since Assad and I had separated he had done a lot of travelling, but whenever he was staying in Sydney he would see the kids once a week. They missed having him living at home with them so much that I called him a few times and asked him to come back and try again, and even asked members of the Afghani community to ask him. But after about eighteen months he sent me divorce papers. I couldn't face the thought of being divorced so I ignored them. Assad sent the papers again. Eventually I signed them and sent them back.

My mum, sisters and brothers said they would come with me to court for the divorce hearing. But when I got a letter from the court telling me the date of the hearing, in May 2000, I kept it to myself. I dropped Tamana off at school and Sourosh at pre-school, and went to court alone.

All I had was my prayer beads. Assad's sister Arozo had married my brother Omar years before, when we were living in Melbourne. For Omar's sake I wanted my divorce to go smoothly, without any arguing between our families, so I thought it best not to involve anyone else.

Sitting there listening to the judge my whole body started aching. When the judge asked Assad if he wanted to divorce me and I heard him say, 'Yes,' my hands started shaking. Drops of sweat fell from my palms onto the table top like water. I realised that I did need somebody beside me, to hold my hand at least. The judge asked if I had any objections to the divorce and I said, 'No,' but I had to struggle to say the word. It brought me pain, like grief for the dead.

Before the hearing Assad and I had politely said hello to each other. Afterwards, though, we passed each other without saying a word. I went past him, got into my car in the parking lot and closed the door. Then I shouted and screamed really loud, so loud that I thought all the planets and stars in the sky must know about it. And then I cried very hard for an hour or so.

Zarmina called me on my mobile and when she heard my voice she asked me what was wrong. When I told her I'd been to court and gotten divorced she was worried about me. 'Why didn't you tell me so I could go with you? Where are you?' I told her I was okay and that she shouldn't worry. But I wasn't okay. I drove home, took a sleeping tablet and went to bed. I wanted to block everything out.

~

My fears about being branded a bad woman by the Afghani community after being divorced turned out to have no basis. No-one made life difficult for me. No-one held the divorce against me. Things were different in Australia: the community had grown to accept divorce. They showed me the same respect they always had, and a lot of empathy. Their support made me feel better about myself. I was a good woman even though I was a divorced woman.

While my marriage had been breaking down Afghanistan had been descending further into hell. In Afghanistan it is not part of the tradition for a woman to be the breadwinner of the house – when a child loses their father they are immediately called an orphan, even if their mother is still alive. Many men had been killed fighting and often their widows had no family left to go to for financial support: they may have fled the country, been killed by war, sickness or starvation, or had their homes destroyed in the fighting. Even if these women could have worked there were no jobs anyway. Their children begged in the streets, picked through garbage looking for something to eat, and slept on the footpath or in destroyed buildings. The orphans who had neither a mother nor a father were even worse off.

The Taliban had control of most of the country but there was still fighting between them and anti-Taliban Mujaheddin. To make matters worse, in 1999 a severe drought set in that would last for about five years. Many people became refugees within their own country, heading to other areas where they hoped there might be more food and water, and less fighting. Millions fled the country altogether. There were about three million Afghanis living in crowded refugee camps near the borders with Pakistan and Iran. Life was appalling in the camps. Jalozai camp, in Peshawar in Pakistan, was probably the worst and was home to about eighty thousand Afghanis. Some of them had been there for so long that they had built poor mudbrick houses to live in. Of the newcomers, a lucky few received tents from aid agencies; the rest did their best to make shelters out of sticks and sheets of plastic, canvas or any other material they could find. Whole families were living in tents that, in the West, we wouldn't even use on a weekend camping trip. The tents sat on the bare earth.

There was no running water, electricity or other services. Parts of the camp were low-lying and often flooded when it rained; then sewage overflowed from the makeshift toilets, spreading disease. In summer the weather was unbearably hot and people died of dehydration. In winter many froze to death. There were no jobs, and there wasn't enough food from the aid agencies to go around. Dr Nasrin was doing everything she could for the thirty-five orphans I sent money over for each month, but I was overwhelmed when I thought about how many thousands of orphans weren't getting any help at all.

In 2000 my Uncle Haji and Aunt Rona, who were retired and in their sixties, travelled from Brisbane to Peshawar for their youngest son's wedding. He was getting married to an Afghani woman and would return with her to Australia, while Uncle Haji and Aunt Rona continued on to Saudi Arabia to undertake the hajj. This is a holy pilgrimage that all Muslims are supposed to make at least once in their lives, if they have enough money and are in good health. During a five-day period each year about two million Muslims from around the world make the pilgrimage, which involves performing a number of rituals in the holy city of Mecca and the surrounding area. Every Muslim dreams of making the hajj and many spend their whole lives saving to make the trip which, from Australia, costs thousands of dollars.

In Peshawar, Uncle Haji and Aunt Rona were saddened by the way Afghani refugees were living. Their situation was much worse than when we were refugees there. Back then, other countries had been sending aid but now there was very little coming in.

At the bazaar near to where my aunt and uncle were staying a man was trying to sell his children because he couldn't afford to feed them. In Peshawar at the time there were many cases of this. Uncle Haji and Aunt Rona discussed the situation and decided to give the money that they were going to spend on the hajj to this man instead, so that he could keep his family together.

Uncle Haji couldn't walk away from what he had seen and go back to his comfortable life in Brisbane. He decided that it was more important for him to stay in Peshawar and try to help the refugee children in the camps. It was a big sacrifice. His two daughters and three sons were grown up now and could look after themselves, but he would miss them, and his ten grandchildren. At first he lived in

Peshawar alone, without even his wife, who returned to Australia, but eventually Aunt Rona too would sacrifice everything and join Uncle Haji.

I have always loved my Uncle Haji. He is a very soft man, with a long white beard. I've never heard him fight with anyone, have never heard him raise his voice. He is a gentle father and a very kind uncle. Sometimes he tries to be tough but it doesn't look right on him. Softness suits him better. Uncle Haji is a spiritual man, who practises his religion from his heart.

I heard through my family that Uncle Haji was living in Peshawar, and that he was doing volunteer work for a charity, helping to run a bakery that provided free bread for Afghani refugees. I started to send four hundred dollars a month to support the bakery, as well as continuing to send money for Dr Nasrin's orphans. After four or five months Uncle Haji and I started to work separately to the charity and organised for another bakery to provide free bread to refugees.

On the phone Uncle Haji and I talked about the desperate need for schools in Jalozai refugee camp. There were very few free schools for refugees, and they couldn't afford to go to the Pakistani schools. A whole generation was missing out on knowing even how to read and write. Uncle Haji had made lots of contacts in Peshawar and people knew that he was interested in helping children get an education. He was offered a piece of land on which to build a school. But he needed thousands of dollars to build it and offer the children free education.

By this time I had started to fundraise in a more organised way – I wasn't just selling off my own things any more. I held a big fundraising event at Granville and about two hundred members of the Afghani community came. There was Afghani singing and food, which some Afghani women I knew cooked for free. Everyone was deeply affected when I read out the children's letters thanking me for helping them and giving them hope. We raised $2,500 that night.

I knew that I would have to raise much more money than that if Uncle Haji was to build a school. A few months after the fundraiser at Granville I organised another, this time at a big function hall in Parramatta. It was mostly for the Afghani community, but a few of my Aussie friends came, too. We had food and singing again, but this time we auctioned a lot of items, such as Afghani bedspreads and Persian rugs, and I managed to raise $10,000. I was overjoyed. I sent $2,000 to Dr Nasrin for the orphans, and $8,000 to Uncle Haji for the school.

Uncle Haji's sons also sent donations to their father to help build the school, and would continue to send money for the running of it long after it was built. Many suppliers in Peshawar gave Uncle Haji building materials for free, and people donated their time to help with the building work. Uncle Haji himself worked on the building site. Within only three months the school was built. It was named Sabit School, Sabit being part of Uncle Haji's surname.

When the school opened, four hundred eager boys seven to thirteen years of age turned up. We only took enrolments from boys at first because some people weren't familiar with the idea of girls going to school and we wanted to ensure we started out with the community's support. Later on, we would open the school to girls as well. The classrooms were very basic. There was no furniture, just some carpet on the floor for the boys to sit on. One wall of each classroom had a patch of blackboard paint applied to it so that the teachers could write on it. Uncle Haji bought the boys some textbooks and stationery. Because they didn't have chairs or desks they either wrote on their laps or leant their book on the back of the boy in front of them. There were window frames but no glass in the windows yet. They mightn't have had many facilities but the boys were very happy because at last they were able to learn something instead of sitting around the camp all day. There were about thirty children in each classroom and fourteen teachers, all young Afghani refugee men who had been among the lucky few to receive an education. They taught the boys all the usual school subjects, such as physics, chemistry, maths, geography and history – and Arabic, religious studies and art.

A few months after the school had opened, when it was running well and proving popular with the community, Uncle Haji had a flyer printed up offering girls the opportunity to come and enrol. We thought a lot of people might be against sending their girls to school, so we expected that at first perhaps fifty or sixty girls would come to enrol and we would gradually build up from there. But two hundred and fifty girls turned up – beautiful girls aged about seven to thirteen – excited at the prospect of being able to learn.

It wasn't seen to be appropriate for the boys and girls to mix so in the morning the boys would come for classes and leave at lunchtime. When all the boys and their male teachers were gone the girls and nine new female teachers would come in and start their classes. The opening of Sabit School was an amazing achievement by my uncle. It wouldn't have been possible without his willingness to fight for the rights of the refugee children.

I called Uncle Haji and suggested we set up some kind of business in Pakistan that would make some money for the children at Sabit School. Uncle Haji said there was a big spare room in the corner of the school building that could be converted into a business. Using money that I had raised in Australia he bought chocolate-making machinery and turned the spare room into a chocolate factory. Uncle Haji set it up like a small business, providing work for the families of several of the children at the school. It turned out that it didn't take the pressure off me to keep raising money, but it gave at least a few refugee families the chance to have a normal life.

The various Afghani ethnic groups tended to cluster together in different sections of the camp. The school was open to children from any ethnic group – we didn't care who they were, they all deserved an education. But because the school was situated in a largely Pashtun area most of the boys and girls were Pashtun, the biggest ethnic group in Afghanistan.

Next, Uncle Haji wanted to help about a hundred and seventy boys aged from around five to eight who had been attending a school in Jalozai camp, in a predominantly Uzbek area. Classes had stopped because they couldn't afford to keep paying the teachers' wages. I sent money over to help Uncle Haji reopen the school and hire five teachers.

The two schools would need a continuous flow of money to pay for the teachers' wages, textbooks and pens and paper, and I was still supporting thirty-five orphans through Dr Nasrin. I had taken on a big responsibility. I'd made a promise to help these children. I thought of them like they were my own; it was as though finding the money to feed, clothe and educate them had become part of the normal running of my household. I didn't see myself as a fundraiser but as a mother to an ever-growing number of children. Sometimes it was hard to sleep at night because I was worried I mightn't be able to raise enough money. I was starting to panic.

Luckily, around this time I met six wonderful people in the Sydney Iranian community who were to become very important to my work. I met a woman named Faroz at Mariam's Sunday class. She and her husband, Mosen, knew it was now vital that I raise $2,000 each month. If I wasn't going to make it they would donate enough money to cover the shortfall. Faroz was a selfless volunteer – she taught me the beauty of doing charity work silently, without asking for acknowledgment. She didn't want any reward or public recognition. The two of us working together – she an Iranian Shia Muslim and me an Afghani Sunni Muslim – reinforced that it was possible to be loving and understanding regardless of coming from different backgrounds. Faroz and Mosen and I developed friendships with four other Iranian people: Mariam and her husband, Mohammed Hagdoosti, and Parisa and her husband, Mohammed Kevianpor. I had no idea just how important their support was about to become.

# Chapter 14

With the devastating attack on the World Trade Center in New York City on September 11, 2001, enormous upheaval came once again to Afghanistan. In the days following the attack it seemed inevitable that the US would bomb and occupy Afghanistan. Many thousands of Afghanis fled the country immediately after September 11, and thousands more when America and its allies started bombing in early October 2001. Neighbouring countries had closed their borders. Tens of thousands of people were stranded on the Afghani side of the border, and new refugee camps sprang up in areas where there was a risk of fighting. There was a humanitarian disaster unfolding.

It was the first time since the end of the Soviet occupation that we had seen much news about Afghanistan on the

TV. Afghanistan had suffered nearly twenty years of civil war since then and we had seen and heard little about it – now every time I turned on the TV or radio it was all about Afghanistan. One of the effects of the media's sudden interest was that to many people Afghanistan now equalled terrorism. Members of the Afghani community in Australia were scared to say where they came from.

Actually, no matter what country we came from, all Muslim Australians were really hurt by September 11. Some women stopped wearing their headscarves because they couldn't stand people calling them names and staring at them on the train or in the street. They were scared they might be attacked. No-one will ever make me take off my headscarf. I did it when I was young, but now that I'm older and stronger there is no power in the world that can make me take it off. After September 11 I got stared at a lot. For the first time since I arrived in Australia I started to experience racism. One day I was waiting in my car for a man to pull out of a parking spot in Auburn, in western Sydney. He saw my scarf and started abusing me, using the F word, and moved his car to block me from driving into the spot so that some people in another car could take it. I drove off straight away: he looked so full of hatred I was scared he might ram me with his car. I started crying. I thought, 'Why should we suffer this much? Why are people doing this to us?'

The growing fear and distrust of Muslims in Australia itself became a news story. A producer at ABC TV's *7.30 Report*, Deb Masters, called a volunteer community worker

I knew, Paula, and told her that the program wanted to interview normal Afghani families, to show their side of the story. Paula told her to call me, hoping that I could find families for the ABC to interview. While we were on the phone Deb happened to ask about my background and what I did. When I told her about the work I was doing with Uncle Haji and Dr Nasrin she suggested that rather than me finding families for her to interview, she should do a story about me and my work.

I agreed to do the story, but when Deb sent me the list of questions that the interviewer would ask I had second thoughts. I wasn't sure how to answer some of the questions, and I was a bit wary of the whole thing because people had told me that you couldn't trust the media. I had never been on TV before and I wasn't sure that it was a good idea. My view was that I was doing my fundraising work for the people of Afghanistan, not for public notice. I was scared that if I started making appearances in the media it might change me; that the purity and simplicity of the way I worked might be spoiled. I believed in God so much that I thought I didn't need publicity – if I had faith in God then people would donate money. But my friend Margaret, who is a strong Christian, argued that God would want me to develop my work a step further: if I talked to the media more people would hear about me and donate money – and then I could help more refugees.

Deb Masters and a film crew and a journalist, Rebecca Baillie, came to my house a few times to interview me. My wariness disappeared as soon as I met Deb and Rebecca.

I could tell straight away that their intentions were positive. It was different to anything I'd ever done before: they filled up my lounge room with lights and cameras, got me to put on make-up, and asked me to keep repeating things so that they could get better shots. I didn't feel nervous having a camera on me – in fact I felt very calm – because all I was thinking about was helping the kids.

An ABC foreign correspondent, Michael Maher, had interviewed Dr Nasrin in Peshawar, and Deb played a tape of the footage on the VCR in my living room. I had seen photos of Dr Nasrin and the orphans but this was the first time that I had seen a video of them. I knew that Dr Nasrin was a very pretty young woman from her photo, but when I saw her speaking to the camera, so modest and gentle, I realised just how beautiful she was. The children were very polite and well behaved, waiting their turn as one of Dr Nasrin's family members who worked with her as a volunteer called them by name and handed them envelopes of cash I had sent from Australia.

I started to cry. The children had such serious little faces – the faces of children who'd seen things even adults shouldn't. The journalist had asked Dr Nasrin to persuade some of the children to tell their stories. It was heartbreaking to hear her say the children's names and translate their words: a young teenage girl looked shyly at the camera, trying to cover her face, and told Dr Nasrin that her father had been killed in fighting, her mother had died in childbirth, there was no-one left in their family to look after her and her sisters and brothers. After I'd watched the video they filmed me answering questions from Rebecca about how it had felt to see the children. It was hard to answer because I was so emotional. Seeing the orphans receiving the money I sent had given me a sense of achievement – I'd made a change in their lives – but I felt overwhelmed that I couldn't do more for them.

When the story aired on the *7.30 Report* I sat down to watch it at home with Tamana and Sourosh, and told the rest of my family that it was on. I was pleased with the way the story came across. It showed Australia another face of Muslim women, more positive than what we were used to seeing on TV. Sourosh was excited when he saw himself helping me to count coins and playing with Margaret's son at the park. Tamana was embarrassed at first to see herself on the screen, but eventually she, like Sourosh, would grow to be proud of the story. Quite a lot of footage of Dr Nasrin made it into the program and I was happy because now people could see that their money really was going to the orphans. There had been a lot in the news about the government putting refugee boat people into detention – the government called these people queue jumpers. At the end Kerry O'Brien came back on and said, 'Some of these children remember no life other than that of a refugee camp. I wonder if *they* understand what a queue is.'

After the story aired on the *7.30 Report* I received hundreds of telephone calls. People got my number from the ABC and rang to make donations, or offer to do volunteer work, or just to wish me well. I didn't have an answering machine so I had to answer the phone every time it rang. I couldn't cope so Margaret came over to my house every day to give me a break. She would answer the phone for a while so that I could go and have a cup of tea or something to eat.

The *7.30 Report* interview was a turning point. The response from the public amazed me and filled me with hope. Hundreds of ordinary Australians cared about the refugee widows and orphans of Afghanistan and wanted to help. Every day in the post cheques arrived. I had about ten volunteers helping me take people's donations, write thank-you letters and plan fundraising events like dinners and public talks.

With more people helping me I was able to raise money at a rate I had never managed to before. I was amazed at what could be achieved when people banded together.

It meant that Uncle Haji and Dr Nasrin could help more people – but it also presented a lot of challenges. I was good at speaking to people about why they should help Afghanistan's children and widows and I was good at asking people to donate money, but I didn't have a clue about running an office, or the rules and regulations for fundraising organisations. I thought that if I was sending every cent we raised to Uncle Haji and Dr Nasrin, and could show records of exactly how the money was spent in Afghanistan and Pakistan, then everything was okay, but actually I needed to have an Authority to Fundraise from the New South Wales Government. I had to put in an application and fulfil all sorts of requirements: I had to have a committee that met regularly and a constitution, a formal statement of why we were raising money.

I didn't know where to start. Nadia, a friend of mine who had done volunteer work for me, was studying to become a solicitor. She introduced me to two solicitors at one of the big law firms, Allens Arthur Robinson. I went and met David and Jenni at their office in a tall building in the city and they agreed to help me for free. Together with my Iranian friend Mohammed Hagdoosti they worked out what I needed to do to get the Authority, filled in the paperwork and advised me on what steps I had to take next.

I had to form a committee, and it was natural that I would ask Mohammed Hagdoosti and my five other Iranian friends who had been helping me for some time now. They named me the president and filled the other official roles themselves, such as vice president, treasurer and secretary. Mohammed Kevianpor wrote a constitution with help from the lawyers and another Iranian friend of his who had written one for an organisation in the past. We named ourselves International Women's and Children's Support Services.

❀

Meanwhile, on the other side of the world, amongst all the horror and misery of 2001 there had also been hope. Order was finally restored to Kabul by the middle of November and Uncle Haji and I saw an opportunity to bring about something good out of the tragedy of that year. In recent times international aid to Afghanistan had dried up and the distribution of whatever aid that had entered the country was often disrupted by fighting – but now Uncle Haji could enter Afghanistan and try to help.

He had been watching the news closely from Peshawar. When he heard that Kabul was safe he set off to his hometown. The refugee schools were running smoothly by now. The principals knew what to do. Uncle Haji would be able to talk to them regularly on the phone and would only have to travel back to Peshawar every now and then to make sure everything was okay.

Nothing could have prepared him for what he saw. The old Kabul was gone. Only about a quarter of the buildings were still standing. The rest were bombed out. The electricity went on and off all the time, and clean water was in short supply because the drought was still dragging on. The people of Kabul were traumatised, hungry, injured and sick. There were homeless children on the streets begging for something to eat. It was even worse than the refugee camps in Peshawar.

Uncle Haji had left behind two houses when he fled the Russian occupation: the one next to mine in Shahr-e-now when I was a little girl, and another in Khair Khana. Luckily they hadn't been hit by bombs. Uncle Haji's children sent him over some money so that he could repaint the houses and do some minor repairs. He moved into the top floor of the house in Khair Khana after buying some new furniture – it had all gone while he was out of the country.

Uncle Haji walked into an emergency situation – people were starving and dying and desperately needed bread in their mouths. He helped one or two widows and orphans in the local area and the word spread quickly. Soon destitute women and children were queuing up at his house. I started to send more money to Uncle Haji so that he could give them handouts of cash, sugar, flour and fuel on a certain day each month.

Uncle Haji also kept careful records of the people he gave help to, taking their names and thumbprints, and sending them to me. One day when I was looking at them I got the idea to run our own sponsorship program, similar to the ones run by charities such as World Vision. Mariam and her husband, Mohammed Hagdoosti, offered to set up the program and administer it. We asked people to contribute thirty-five dollars a month, and in return sent them photos and fingerprints of their sponsored children or widows, showing that they had received the money. Sometimes the children and widows would write their sponsor a thank-you note, or would tell them about their life. Sometimes sponsors would send letters or packages of donated goods and we would forward them on to their sponsored widows and children.

Once Uncle Haji had the emergency relief under way he turned his attention to other types of assistance. He and I had often discussed how the best way to help people is to help them get an education and training so that they can support themselves for the rest of their lives. He decided that he would devote the downstairs section of his house in Khair Khana to doing just that. We talked about what kind of training could help the many young women of Kabul who had missed out on getting any sort of education and were struggling to survive. We came up with the idea of offering sewing classes because sewing was something that was familiar to Afghani women and something they could earn their living from.

I raised some money and sent it to Uncle Haji, and he bought ten sewing machines and had them installed in the ground floor of his house. He employed a woman who could teach sewing and within only a few weeks the classes began, and the first class of girls learnt how to make clothes and do fine embroidery.

Uncle Haji and I had a dream to start an orphanage to get at least some of Kabul's homeless children off the streets. The problem was finding a building to house the orphans. The ones that were still standing attracted very high rents. Uncle Haji offered his house in Shahr-e-now but I didn't want him to make yet another personal sacrifice. He had already given up so much. But he kept raising it with me – he must have mentioned it three or four times. Eventually I understood just how committed he was to giving up his own home, and I agreed. A few minor alterations would need to be made to the house to make it suitable, and we would have to buy a lot of new furnishings, and employ staff. That would mean raising more money. But it couldn't be just a one-off big fundraiser: we would need to secure a continuous stream of funding to feed and clothe the children, give them an education and employ staff to look after them. Once we took the children off the streets we would be committed to being their family, to never letting them down. It would take my volunteers and me time to come up with enough money for that. Some nights I couldn't sleep thinking of the beautiful orphanage we would one day have in Uncle Haji's house.

~

I had become the president of an official fundraising organisation but I didn't even know what a minute was. At our committee meetings each month I kept thinking, 'Minute? One minute, ten minutes?' It was a while before I worked out that they were talking about the record Mohammed Hagdoosti made of what was said at each meeting. My dining table was piled high with papers because I didn't have a filing cabinet. I didn't even have a computer until Mohammed Hagdoosti bought one and set it up for me. A fax machine was donated to me, and an answering machine, which was great because now I didn't have to be at home all the time but could go out fund-raising or giving talks about our work. I was even given a second-hand photocopier.

I needed an office to fit all this equipment in but didn't want to pay rent for one because it would mean less money going to the widows and orphans. My garage was filled with old things we didn't need any more. I cleaned everything out and packed up any useful goods and sent them to Afghanistan for Uncle Haji to give to widows and orphans. I had some tiles laid on the floor of the garage, got some furniture and turned the garage into an office.

The volunteers who helped with fundraising and administration could only come in every now and then – a few hours here, a few hours there – because they all led busy lives and most had jobs. They needed me to tell them where to save documents in the computer or where to file hard copies of letters and receipts, and how to update our list of donors, because otherwise it was hard for the other volunteers to find things. It was like the blind leading the blind: I had hardly any idea about office work but I had to take the hands of the volunteers and try to show them our system.

My family's house wasn't really our house any more – it was an office. People would come at all hours, from first thing in the morning until ten or eleven at night. We had no more private life but I didn't mind. I was just glad to find that so many people cared and wanted to help. And my volunteers were the nicest, warmest people I could hope to have around my house. Several of them developed good friendships with Tamana and Sourosh, even helping them with school work sometimes.

I invited new volunteers to come to committee meetings, and more and more of them joined the committee. Soon we had people with fundraising expertise; marketing, publicity and journalism backgrounds; accounting skills and administration experience. With their help the organisation began to really take shape. The original group of Iranian committee members eventually had to step down from their roles as office bearers when things got too busy, and other people took their places. Faroz and Mosen are now living in Iran, Parisa and Mohammed Kevianpor have started a family but help out when they get a chance, and Mariam and Mohammed Hagdoosti are still regular volunteers.

One thing that seemed to be holding us back was our name. It was too hard for people to remember International Women's and Children's Support Services let alone write it on a cheque. The other committee members believed that if the organisation was to grow we had to develop a strong identity, so we had a meeting to decide on a new name. Our vice president, Marie, suggested that we should be called Mahboba's Promise. I wasn't sure about including my own name in the title as so many people were working hard, not just me. But everyone on the committee agreed with Marie. They thought the name summed up what we were all about: a promise to never abandon the widows and orphans of Afghanistan, who had no-one else to turn to.

# Chapter 15

In 2002, I and some of the committee members decided to go overseas and see for ourselves how our programs were going. I had mixed feelings. It had been two decades since I left Afghanistan. I wanted to go back and see the familiar landscapes and the home where I had grown up. My heart ached to walk down the street and hear people speaking my language, to eat the Afghani food I had known when I was a child, to be surrounded by the customs and culture I had been brought up with. But at the same time I doubted that I had enough money to take with me: I knew the kind of terrible poverty I would see. Perhaps it would be better to wait a little longer and raise more money. What convinced me to go was the sight of the children's faces on the *7.30 Report* – I couldn't get them out of my head. I knew how much the children needed love.

Marie, our vice president, was keen to come with me. I had known her since just after the *7.30 Report* screened. She was at home cleaning up after dinner when the story came on. She rang me soon after and became an important part of Mahboba's Promise; she also had a job as a teacher. I asked one of our most active fundraisers, a woman named Jo, to come along, too. She was leading a peaceful life with her husband of forty years on a lovely farm in the New South Wales countryside – her lifestyle was so different to the way people lived in Afghanistan. Her children were scared about her going and at first she was too, but she did decide to join us. Libby, the secretary of Mahboba's Promise, joined the group, along with a friend and colleague of hers, Lisa. I knew that it would be good to have at least one Dari speaker in the group to take the pressure off me a little – luckily Rose, an Afghani-Aussie girl I knew, was keen to go and visit her family, and she also joined our group.

We knew it would be of great benefit to have the media follow our trip so that the public could also see the good that their donations were bringing. Deb Masters, who had produced the *7.30 Report* story, was keen to do a story for ABC TV's *Australian Story*. While the *7.30 Report* story had been about seven minutes long, this one would run for half an hour. I trusted Deb and was happy for her to come along with a film crew.

We flew out in September 2002, almost a year since the attacks on the World Trade Center in New York City. There was a fear that it might be a dangerous time to travel. The fact that there were Westerners and journalists in our group could also potentially make us a target – Westerners and journalists had been killed and taken hostage in Afghanistan before. We knew that in Kabul things were relatively peaceful but that outside of the capital we would have to be very careful as there was still fighting. Tamana and Sourosh were worried about my safety and it was difficult and emotional to say goodbye to them at the airport. My mother was going to take them to Perth for a holiday with my brother Omar – I knew they were in good hands and I had nothing to worry about, but that didn't mean I wouldn't miss them.

First we flew to Islamabad, the capital of Pakistan, and from there we drove to Peshawar. We had hired two cars and local drivers, and would do so for the remainder of our trip. After the three and a half hour drive we checked into our hotel, dropped off our bags and left again to go and visit Sabit School. On the way to Peshawar I had been feeling hopeful that the situation for the refugees there might have changed for the better. But in the hotel carpark our cars were surrounded by Afghani women and children begging for money. They could tell from our clothes and our well-fed faces that we were from overseas – and that meant we had money. One woman, whose face was covered with a *burqa*, held her baby out towards me and pleaded, 'He is going to die. Please help me, please help me.' Her baby looked about six months old and wasn't moving at all – he looked as though he was so sick that he might even be unconscious. They all started talking about their problems. Their stories were heartbreaking – their husbands were dead; they couldn't find food or medicine for their children; they were watching their children waste away. I couldn't say anything; I just cried.

I had brought money with me from Australia to give to Dr Nasrin and Uncle Haji. In Islamabad I had exchanged quite a lot for Pakistani rupees. The person at the money exchange had given the rupees to me in big bundles of notes that were tied up very tightly. I was scared that if I opened my bag and started untying the bundles of cash and distributing it to the women and children they might attack us and take all the money. They were desperate people. I pulled out one bundle of notes and handed it to the woman with the sick baby. We all rolled our windows up. A few of Uncle Haji's volunteers had come to meet us at the hotel to escort us to Sabit School – they had to shout at the people begging to get them to move so they wouldn't get run over.

I will never forget that woman and her baby, or the other women and their sick and hungry children. I truly wanted to help them but I had to think about our safety. We pulled out of the carpark and the women and children followed our cars down the road for a while, their hands raised, begging for help. It was one of the really horrible moments of my life. Things were just as bad for Afghani refugees as they had been twenty years ago when I lived in Peshawar, and I felt powerless.

It was frightening when we reached the section of Jalozai refugee camp where the school is because there was a checkpoint and a guard armed with a big gun. He demanded to know what our business was in this part of the camp before he would let our car through. When Jo saw the gunman she was so scared she slid down below the seat in front of her. One of Uncle Haji's volunteers got out of the car and explained what we were doing and the guard waved us through. Jalozai was a grim place, and we passed rows and rows of very poorly built mudbrick houses and tents. We saw mothers begging in the street with their children lying on the ground at their feet.

When we got to the school the mood in the car suddenly got a lot brighter: the gates were open and four hundred little boys were standing in a guard of honour on either side of the path, waving Afghani and Australian flags. A stage had been set up out the front of the school building, with a marquee and rows of chairs. The boys were having their speech day and I felt honoured to be there. The best students received awards. Some stood in front of the microphone and gave speeches, sang songs and read poems. They were very respectful and well-behaved and serious-looking – you could tell that they'd been through a lot – but their eyes were shining because they were so happy to be able to perform for us. I thought about all the fundraising I had done to help Uncle Haji build their school. It was worth every moment to see all their little faces. I gave a short speech and told them how amazed and proud I was of their performances on the stage. I told them I knew of their suffering and that I hoped it would end soon and they would be free, just like other children. My Uncle Haji's pride in the boys shone from his face. We were happy to be together again, and were proud of what we had achieved.

After the speeches and songs the boys had lunch. About fifteen volunteers come each day to cook and serve the kids food. For most of them it's the only proper meal they get each day. It takes some of the pressure off families who are struggling to find enough food for their children. The boys went home and two hundred and fifty or so little girls came, had their lunch, and then had their speech day. I was overjoyed that they too could stand in front of the microphone just like experienced public speakers. For an Afghani girl to be confident enough to stand up and perform in front of a crowd is really something. I got up on the stage with some of the girls and sang a song with them. It was an emotional time – it was a song about how much we love Afghanistan and how tired the people of Afghanistan are of suffering.

At both the boys' and girls' assemblies we had handed out school bags and stationery to every child. We had brought coloured pencils from Australia but only had enough to hand out two pencils to each child. A tiny girl came to me empty-handed afterwards and told me she wasn't old enough to start school yet but her sister had brought her along for the day. She told me she'd always dreamed of having a coloured pencil. She looked up at me with big brown eyes and said, 'Can I have one please?' I looked through my bags but couldn't find any. I rushed back to the car and searched everywhere, and finally found one last packet of twelve coloured pencils. I came back and gave her the packet. When I saw from her eyes how happy she was because she had twelve coloured pencils I wanted to cry.

All of us thought Uncle Haji was doing an incredibly good job of running the school. As a teacher, Marie was very impressed with the order and organisation he had created, and with how disciplined and attentive the children were. She was amazed at what he had achieved with so few facilities. Because Uncle Haji had lived in Australia and visited other developed countries he aimed to give the children the same standard of education as Australian children.

We went into one classroom full of girls aged between seven and nine years old who were sitting on the floor. Marie and I asked them if they ever wrote stories. They all said no, they never did. When we asked why, they said that it was because their stories were so sad. I think it's important for kids to feel they can talk about everything, even the bad things that happen in their lives. These kids had been through so much. They needed love and attention; they needed somebody to listen to them, understand them, and help them heal. So we said: 'Is somebody brave enough to come up the front and tell us something about their life?'

A girl came out to the front of the classroom. She was shy and she shook as she told us and her classmates about the night she had a dream in which her father came to her and said, 'I'm dead.' The next day when she was telling her mother about her dream his body was brought to their house: he had been killed in the fighting. She talked about what her father had been like, and started to cry. I put my arm around her and she rested her head on my shoulder. We cried together, and as soon as I started crying, all of these gorgeous girls in the classroom started to cry. They then felt safe and confident enough to start telling their stories of how they survived despite losing family members.

The next day a woman told me about twelve orphans who were in the care of a man and a woman who themselves were very poor and couldn't look after them properly. She took me to visit the children, who were all thin and obviously suffering from hunger. I asked their carers' permission to take the children out for the day and they agreed, so long as the man came along to make sure nothing happened to them. The children all wanted to sit on my lap in the car on the way back to the hotel. I held their hands and hugged them, and they told me their stories, how they had become orphans. We all ended up crying.

Then I said, 'Okay, today is a happy day for you. I want you not to cry any more and I'm going to stop crying. We're going to have fun today.' I asked them to tell me what they wanted to do. They said they hadn't eaten meat for months, and could they have some Afghani kebab. And then they mentioned fruit such as apples and grapes, and clothing, too. Not one child asked me for toys – all they wanted was the bare essentials of food and clothes.

I was going with the other women and the film crew to visit Dr Nasrin that day so I took the orphans with me. Dr Nasrin was now operating out of a childcare centre, which let her use part of the building for free. She had about ten of her family members doing volunteer work. Once a month she would hand out cash to the orphans on her list, and she had expanded her list to include widows as well. She also paid the orphans' school fees. Whenever there was an emergency, such as one of the widows or orphans needing an operation, she would call me and I'd quickly raise some more money to send over to pay for it. I'd also send money over for one-off projects, such as buying a five-hundred-dollar asthma machine for the Afghani refugee hospital, which saved several children's lives each week.

There were about thirty-five orphans standing in a guard of honour to welcome us, just like at the school. They had signs pinned to the front of their clothes that said, in English, things such as 'Mahboba is my mother and my father' and 'We need Mahboba.' I felt overwhelmed.

We had come on the day of the monthly distribution of cash, and Dr Nasrin also had some food and clothing to give each of the widows and orphans. Dr Nasrin arranged for me to hand everything out. She started calling out names from a list and as she called each name a volunteer handed me an envelope of cash and a bundle of goods from the storeroom behind us. I then handed them to the widow or orphan. But the women and children wouldn't wait for their names to be called. They panicked that they might miss out and all rushed forward at the same time. They yelled, 'Give it to me, give it to me.'

I shouted, 'There's enough for every one of you, please sit down. I've come all the way from Australia to see you.' Nobody listened; they kept pushing forward. I was surrounded by women all talking at the same time: 'My children will die', 'My husband's dead, I've had to become a beggar', 'I have no money for medicine for my children.' Little children crowded around me, too.

I did my best to stay calm and distribute the goods and cash, but then I just burst into tears. I had to go away and sit down and have a break. I started hating myself. I felt so guilty. I thought: 'I haven't done my job properly; I haven't made these women happy. I have to do more.'

Libby said to me, 'Mahboba you're only one person. You can only do as much as you can to help people.' Dr Nasrin's husband took over from me and distributed everything and after a while things quietened down. When they had all gotten something they sat down on the ground.

Because of all the chaos it had taken longer to distribute the goods and cash than planned and it was time to go. It was lunchtime and Dr Nasrin had organised a lunch for us and her family at her house. I stood up and said goodbye. The widows came up – more calm and orderly this time – and held my hand and asked if I could just sit and talk for a while. I started crying again and said that I couldn't. I wanted to listen to them but we didn't have any more time. It was sad because if they had come forward one by one I could have listened to their stories. It wasn't their fault: they had panicked because nobody else had ever given them anything or spent time with them.

Dr Nasrin's family members were exactly as I had imagined them: beautiful, honest people. They were totally selfless in the way they helped others and I trusted them

completely. Dr Nasrin and I had built up a strong relationship on the phone but as soon as we saw each other face-
to-face she felt just like a sister to me.

The orphans I had brought along joined us at Dr
Nasrin's while we had lunch, but I went out and bought
them the kebabs and other food that they had asked for.
That afternoon I bought material and took it to a tailor to
make some clothing for them. I spent a quarter of an hour
with each child on my lap or sitting next to me and I gave
them lots of hugs. I spoiled them for one day.

Eventually I had to say goodbye but the kids didn't want
to go. They cried, and I cried. I gave them each some money,
and I gave the man who was in charge of them some money
and said, 'This is for you just to love the children.'

He said to me, 'You're giving me this money just to love
the kids?'

I said, 'Yes. These children not only need food, they need
somebody to love them.'

~

The day after we visited Dr Nasrin it was time to head to
Afghanistan. Uncle Haji had already returned to Kabul,
where we would meet up with him again in a few days.
Our journey was to take us through the Khyber Pass, and
the mountainous tribal areas could be dangerous because
different groups were still fighting for control. In order to
cross we had to get a special permit. When I went to pay for
it I was told that I would be assigned two gunmen to travel

with us. It was one of the requirements for receiving the permit – we would not be allowed to travel without them. I said that I wanted to choose which men would travel with us. I knew that the women in my group would be alarmed about having gunmen with us so I chose two friendly looking men with nice smiles. As I left the building with the gunmen I asked them to give me their guns and I slung one over each shoulder as I walked back to the cars, to show the others that they didn't need to be scared of the men or their weapons.

Nothing could take our fear away when we started our journey across the Khyber Pass, though. There were big signs prohibiting foreigners from entering. We had no trouble getting through, with our permits, but it didn't make it any less scary. I had taught the women in our group how to wear scarves but they weren't used to them and they kept sliding off. And even with scarves on they still stood out because of their fair skin. There were mostly men out on the streets in the villages we passed through, and they all stopped and looked at us. As we approached the border I was filled with an irrational fear: I had escaped my country in secrecy and had believed at the time that it would never be safe for me to return. Even though the Russians were long gone the sense of danger still hung over me.

But as soon as we crossed the Afghanistan border and I saw my country and breathed the cool, fresh air of the mountains my fear was replaced by excitement and joy. The others were all tired, and sick of the jerking movement of

Sourosh at eight months old. He looked a lot
like Arash at the same age.

These are the conditions people live in at the tent city I first saw on my trip to Kabul
in 2003.

Typical Kabul street scenes. After decades of war only about a quarter of the buildings survived.

Dr Nasrin (far right) and me with some of the Peshawar orphan girls.

Many of the children in Jalozai refugee camp, Peshawar, are sick or have skin conditions, like this little boy.

With the girls of Sabit School in Peshawar, 2002.

The boys of Sabit School in Peshawar welcoming me on my visit in 2002. They are holding Australian and Afghani flags.

Happy faces at one of our schools in Jalozai refugee camp, Peshawar.

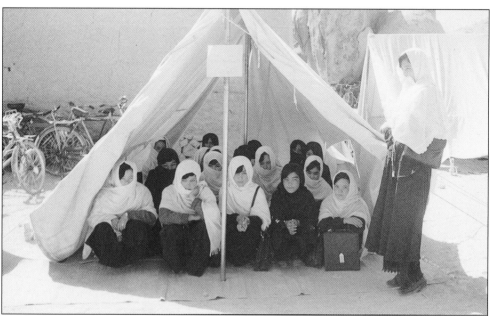

These girls in remote Afghanistan are so desperate for an education that they attend classes in a cramped tent. My goal is to find a sister school in Australia who will help support these students.

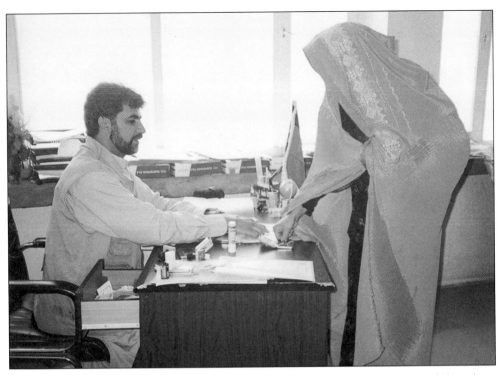

My brother Sidiq in Kabul – this widow is giving her fingerprint, as a record that she has just received a payment from Mahboba's Promise.

Some of the widows and orphans who receive support through our sponsorship program, standing in front of Hope House.

Me and my mother.

Uncle Haji and me on my 2002 trip.

Sourosh, Tamana and me at Tamana's sixteenth birthday party.

the car on the winding road, but every time the car jolted I laughed because I was so happy. When we came to a place where we could stop beside a river I got out and bent down and splashed my face and laughed some more – I didn't care that all my clothes were getting wet.

We stopped when we reached Jalalabad, one of the major cities of Afghanistan, which is close to the Khyber Pass. For six months or so Mahboba's Promise had been sending money there for the schooling of twenty-three orphan girls from seven to thirteen years old. I had always wanted to do something to help girls in Jalalabad because there are not many schools for girls there, and not many opportunities for girls to have a life. Another reason I wanted to do something in Jalalabad is that it is a Pashtun area, while I am a Tajik woman: I wanted to show people who promote divisions and fighting between ethnic groups that there is nothing wrong with helping and living in peace with each other. An Afghani-Australian man in Sydney had put me in contact with a man in Jalalabad who wanted to open a school. The Jalalabad community got behind the project and donated goods and money, and Mahboba's Promise began to send over five hundred dollars a month.

The schoolgirls were really warm. They wanted to sit on our laps and put their heads on our shoulders. They loved it when some of the women told them stories about their lives in Australia. In Afghanistan, to be an orphan and a girl is the worst thing that can happen to you. Your only future might be to beg on the streets. We were only saving twenty-three girls by giving them an education, but if we could save even one girl it would be a good thing.

After visiting the girls in Jalalabad we set out for Kabul. Many people had warned us not to travel on the road to Kabul after dark as we might get caught up in fighting or possibly be kidnapped or murdered, but it was about two in the afternoon and it was only a hundred and fifty kilometres or so to Kabul. We had to drive slowly, though, because the road was just dirt and rocks with huge potholes. We were still on the road when the sun began to set. Then one of the cars got a mechanical problem. There was a feeling of panic among the group. I got the women and the television crew to drive on in the other car to a place where there was lighting, to wait for me. I went back with the driver to the last village we had passed through and got the car fixed. I was really worried about something happening to the others but the car was fixed quickly and we met up with them down the road. We arrived in Kabul about eight hours after leaving Jalalabad.

The next morning we went to Uncle Haji's house at Khair Khana to see the sewing school. I told the driver that I knew the way and would show him. But Kabul looked completely different. It was one thing to hear the reports about how three-quarters of the buildings had been destroyed in the fighting but it was another thing to see it for myself. Nothing was the same as when I had left twenty years before. As we drove through the city I kept thinking, 'Where is Kabul? I'm still waiting to see it.' In the places where once there were shops and restaurants and homes with pretty gardens and flowerbeds I saw wrecked shells of buildings. I couldn't recognise anything. A beautiful park where I had played as a child was nothing but dust and rubble. I felt like I'd gone to another planet. So many landmarks had gone I didn't know where I was and we got lost. There are no phone boxes in Afghanistan; you have to go to a special kind of shop that rents out the use of a phone. We finally found one so we could call Uncle Haji and the driver could get directions to his house.

The week or so that we were in Kabul was full of shocking sights. So many children were out working because their families had no money to feed them otherwise. Everywhere you went you heard children saying, 'Water, water, water,' as they tried to sell bottles of water. Others polished shoes or washed cars, or sold things like chewing gum or socks. A lot of the children had sores or rashes or infected insect bites on their faces and hands.

I think that most of the Australian women were glad to go home because you couldn't see all the poverty and suffering of Afghanistan and not be affected. Rose and I were torn, though. We hadn't seen enough of Kabul; we wanted to keep looking and listening. It was our homeland and we had been separated from it for so long that it was hard to leave. After we had checked our bags in at the airport, we had to go back to the window so we could look out at the people passing by. We saw children selling water to earn a living, while we were about to get on a plane to a place where the children had everything they needed.

'I don't know if we're the lucky ones or they are,' I said to Rose, looking out the window. 'We have food but we're far away from the country where we were born. They have their country but no food.'

~

I never worried about Tamana and Sourosh while I was away because I knew my mother and Omar and Arozo were looking after them, but I missed them very much. They were worried about me, though. There had been US military action in other parts of Afghanistan while we were there. I had rung them to reassure them that there hadn't been any fighting where we were – but still they were relieved when I came home. They showed me a diary that they had written in each day about what they'd done with their cousins, and saying how much they loved and missed me.

I cried every day of my trip and lost six kilos in two weeks. Of course compared to what people in Afghanistan and the refugee camps in Pakistan were going through every day of their lives I hadn't suffered at all. But I would never forget the suffering I had seen. It had made me even more determined to give every minute of the day and every breath in my body to helping Afghani people rebuild their lives after decades of war.

Shortly after I got home from Afghanistan the Bali bombings happened. Eighty-eight Australians were killed. It was so horrible to see violence affecting Australians, so awful to turn on the television and see people losing their lives like that. A couple of days later I was due to give a talk at a fundraiser in Canberra. I was sitting on the platform at Strathfield station in Sydney waiting for the train to Canberra when a man walked past me, glared at me like I was a criminal and said, 'Stupid Muslim, go back to your country.' He sat down near me and stared at me. The station was busy and there were people everywhere but there was no reaction from anyone else. I picked up my bag and went and sat on the other side of the platform to get away from him.

He followed me and sat near me again, still staring at me. For a minute or so I stared back at him. I thought to myself, 'Should I say to him, "Which country should I go back to? I went to my old country, and there is no country there. It has been destroyed".' I wanted to tell him, 'I went to find my home but I could not find my home. *This* is my home.' But I realised that there was no point in me trying to reason with him. His mind was poisoned and it would take more than my words to make him understand. I moved to another seat and he followed me again, but then my train arrived and he had to stay on the platform, waiting for his train.

I was shaken and saddened, but as soon as I arrived at the fundraising event in Canberra my worries about what had happened at the train station disappeared because there were about two hundred influential people there – including many politicians and ambassadors – who treated me like a queen. Someone took me by the hand and walked me to the stage. The crowd listened with respect to my speech about what I had seen on my trip to Afghanistan, and altogether they donated $20,000. On the way home I thought to myself, 'There are so many good, understanding people that it doesn't matter if one or two, or ten or a hundred,do not understand you.' I prayed for the man who had harassed me at the station. One day he will understand that refugees have no choice but to leave their birthplace, and that we love our new country. Australia *is* home for us.

The purpose of the big fundraiser in Canberra had been to buy medical equipment for a clinic that Uncle Haji had built in my mother's village, Abdara, in Panjshir Valley. It had long been a dream of my mother's for her village to have a school and a doctor. Abdara had a population of about one and a half thousand people but no medical services and only a boys' school. I had shared my mother's dream since the holy month of Ramadan years before. There is a night towards the end of Ramadan that is considered to be the most holy night of all the year and many people spend it at the mosque. I was beside my mother at the mosque reading from the Holy Book Qur'an with everyone else, following along with the sheikh. My mother wasn't, though. There were tears running down her cheeks. Afterwards I asked her why she had been crying and she told me that it was because she couldn't read and join in. 'You are so lucky you can read and write,' she'd said. It was then I knew that one day I had to help educate little girls in Abdara. My mother also wished the girls and women of Abdara could finally have access to a doctor and medicine.

Over the years I had come to know and trust the people at another charity organisation, Muslim Aid Australia, who give help to Muslims in need anywhere in the world. They have the same outlook and way of working as me. I had asked them to support the project and they had donated $20,000. This, plus further money I had raised, had been enough to allow Uncle Haji to begin building works. When Uncle Haji went to the community and said what we wanted to do they were very grateful and donated some communally owned land on which to build a school and medical centre.

Finding the money for the medical centre and school, and a place to build them, turned out to be the easy part. Abdara was a remote village two and a half hours' drive from Kabul. It was a very poor place and there were no building materials available there. Every brick, every piece of timber, every tile, every pane of glass had to be brought from Kabul. The road was rough and rocky, and was only wide enough for one truck. It was cut into the side of the mountains and down below was the Panjshir River. It was hard to find a driver who would take you along that road.

The villagers had to walk across fields and up a mountain each day to get drinking water from a spring. The builders had to haul water up from the river to get water to mix their concrete and cement. But perhaps the greatest challenge of all was that the land we had been given was on the side of a mountain. It had to be levelled before building work could even commence.

At the beginning Uncle Haji employed Abdara men as workers so that the money would stay in the village. They weren't experienced in building, though, and the project ran into a lot of problems; some of the work had to be knocked down and done again. Finally Uncle Haji had to hire construction workers from Kabul and bring them to Abdara, where they usually camped rather than travelling back and forth each day.

One day Uncle Haji was returning from Kabul to Abdara when his driver lost control and went off the road, down the side of a mountain. A big boulder stopped their fall but the car landed upside down. People who witnessed the crash ran to help them out of the car and back up the road to safety. Uncle Haji was okay but one of the workers who was in the car got a broken leg.

When I heard how hard it was for Uncle Haji sometimes I wanted to give up, but a voice inside me always said, 'No, we have to make it, we have to succeed.' And after only six months the bulk of the building work was done. Once I had raised enough money to pay for equipment and staff we could open the school and medical centre, and my mother's dream would come true.

# Chapter 16

By July 2003 Uncle Haji's house in Shahr-e-now was almost ready to have orphans move in so I flew to Afghanistan again, to help him open it. People in Australia had donated lots of things that the orphans would need, like toothbrushes, soap, towels and clothes – it filled ten suitcases. I took hardly anything for myself because I wanted to fill up my bags with things for the orphans: all I packed was one cotton dress and a pair of shoes. Even though my luggage was way over the weight limit, once Singapore Airlines knew what I was carrying they didn't charge me. This time I travelled on my own because I wanted to be able to focus all of my attention on the orphans. I flew via Singapore and Dubai to Kabul airport, where Uncle Haji was waiting for me.

I was so excited when he showed me what he had done to his house. There would be room for up to fifty orphans. Downstairs there were two big rooms that would be used during the day as a living area while at night the boys would sleep on the floor on mattresses. The girls would use two similar-sized rooms upstairs as their bedroom. Downstairs Uncle Haji had converted a small living room into a library for all the children to use. Upstairs he had turned another small room into an office. He had built an extension onto the side of the house for a big kitchen and dining room. I had asked Uncle Haji to buy the best of everything, so there were fine Persian rugs and curtains, brand new pillows, mattresses and bedding, a fridge and freezer, tables and chairs. The house looked fit for the President of Afghanistan to live in. We didn't want the children to feel like orphans.

I spent the first few days of my trip registering Mahboba's Promise as an NGO, or non-governmental organisation, in Afghanistan. It was necessary to achieve NGO status if we were to operate an orphanage and open a bank account in Afghanistan in the organisation's name. It takes a long time to do anything official in Afghanistan because most offices, even in government departments and banks, have little equipment. Just finding a photocopier is hard. The process of registering as an NGO normally takes months but I would only be in Afghanistan for three weeks. We had to open the orphanage during my stay – there were children depending on us. I explained the urgency of the situation to people in the Foreign Affairs Department, which administers NGOs, and asked them to help me. I sat in their offices and wouldn't leave until I had the signatures or paperwork I needed. When they heard about what I was trying to do for the orphans, and saw how determined I was, they put a lot of effort into helping me; some people even worked overtime. Mahboba's Promise was a registered NGO in Afghanistan within three days.

Uncle Haji had already selected a shortlist of people for jobs at the orphanage and I spent a day with him interviewing them. We needed a cleaner, a cook and a carer to make sure the children were bathed every day and had clean clothes to wear, and to look after them if they were sick. Although the children would go to a nearby school we also wanted a teacher to come and tutor them outside school hours and help them with their homework. We chose the most calm, honest, trustworthy women, and sent a few away because they weren't warm and friendly enough. We had to be able to trust that they would look after the kids as if they were their own.

Uncle Haji already had a list of orphans who would move into the orphanage. The first to arrive were ten children from Panjshir Valley, who we paid someone to drive down to Kabul. They were well behaved, shy and quiet when they arrived. I welcomed them to their new home and sat down and chatted with them for a while. Their skin was dry and had cuts and sores on it, so I rubbed cream and disinfectant in where they needed it. I asked them what they wanted to be and they all had big dreams. They wanted to be doctors, solicitors, teachers, businesspeople. All of them had poor, worn-out shoes and rough-looking feet so I gave them each two pairs of socks, some clothing and a toothbrush. Everything was brand new, from Australia. Happy and smiling, they put their socks on straight away. I would later have to teach them how to brush their teeth because they'd never had toothbrushes before.

Another ten orphans moved in gradually over the next few days – some of them were on Uncle Haji's list, others I had found begging on the streets. They were happy to have a beautiful home and lots of other children to play with, but because they had all been living such hard lives they had some problems, too. The orphans had gotten used to struggling just to have a meal each day and they weren't used to being given things. At every meal they gorged themselves. When they saw food they ate as much as they could in case they weren't going to get another meal for a long time. Gradually they came to learn that they didn't have to gorge; we weren't going to let them go hungry. Some of the children broke windows and fought with each other until they had got used to their surroundings and calmed down. And when we had clothes and other goods to hand out they would fight over them because they thought they might miss out otherwise. We had to teach them to wait their turn and had to reassure them that they weren't going to be left out.

Most days I was busy doing other Mahboba's Promise work outside the orphanage. One day when I went back, some of the children from Panjshir Valley were sad and homesick. I put on some Afghani music and stood up and showed them how to do exercises, like star jumps. They'd never done exercises before and they thought it was really funny. The mood started to change and soon the kids began singing and dancing and reading poems. Pretty soon they'd cheered up. The woman we had employed as their tutor started crying. She had been trying for days to get them to cheer up.

I was overcome seeing the children playing and laughing in my uncle's old house that I had run around and played in as a child. My family had lived next door but it felt as though our uncles' houses had been our homes; we were always running in and out to visit our cousins. Now a new generation of children, who, until only days before had had nothing, were able to enjoy my uncle's home.

Uncle Haji's house still had an old-fashioned pit toilet out in the yard. There were no showers so to bathe you heated up water and splashed yourself using a bucket. As the orphanage was eventually going to house fifty children we decided it was time to install modern Western-style toilets and showers upstairs and downstairs. Of course that meant we would need running water, which the house didn't have; there was a pump and a well out the front of the house. Once the plumbers had fixed everything, after I left Kabul, the kids were able to have showers and use a modern toilet for the first time in their lives. But Uncle Haji told me there was still a big line outside the old-style toilet. The new Western-style toilet looked weird to them; they weren't used to sitting up on something to do their business. Eventually they got used to using the new toilets and showers inside, but there are still some children who prefer to use the toilet outside and wash with buckets of water.

The staff did their jobs well and the children were washed, dressed, fed and schooled. The challenge I faced was getting them to look after the children emotionally. People in Afghanistan have seen so many bad things that their hearts have become like stone. It's hard for them to feel sorry for an orphan who is lucky enough to be in an orphanage and have the kind of food, toys and clothing that Australian kids have.

Some nights I stayed in the orphanage and sat down and let the children get on my lap two at a time, brushing their hair and making sure their faces and hands were clean. They weren't used to being shown affection so at first they shrank away, trembling, but slowly they got used to it and liked it. I told them they were beautiful and precious, and that I would be there for them in the night if they needed me. They became calm and happy, and it was easy to get them off to sleep then. They hadn't had anyone to love them for a long time, and they needed it. The orphanage workers were good women but they had been through a lot; they had nothing left to give. When they saw me treating the children tenderly they actually started to cry.

We had one staff member who would do the same for the children after I returned to Australia: a sixteen-year-old orphan girl named Latifah. She had been coming monthly to receive money from Uncle Haji and I had met her on my first trip back to Afghanistan when I'd gone to interview the women that Uncle Haji was helping. She was hysterical, screaming and crying about the day that her father and brother were both killed in a rocket attack. She was the one who had found their bodies and been responsible for bringing them home and burying them. Their bodies were blown apart and Latifah had never been able to find one of her father's legs. She couldn't forgive herself for burying him that way. Her story had disturbed me so much I recorded it and it was played on SBS radio during their Afghani program. We employed Latifah in the orphanage and she is still working there as a wonderful carer for the other orphans. She understands how they feel and what they need.

I knew that I could rely on Latifah to give the children love but Latifah couldn't be there all the time. We already had a nightshift worker to cook and clean and make sure the children were safe and well, but the children also needed someone who could focus on making them feel loved.

I asked Uncle Haji what he thought about employing a woman to come each night just to sit with the children and read them a story and make them feel loved and protected, then stay overnight so the children could come to her if they were scared or sick. The difficulty was finding a woman who could work night shift, as most men weren't happy to have their wives do that. After I left Kabul Uncle Haji employed a widow for the job.

~

On my first trip to Kabul I was horrified by how many children I saw in the streets begging, washing cars, or selling things like plastic bags, umbrellas and shoe polish. In the second week of my trip I left the house at about six each morning with one of my relatives, who drove me in his car around the streets of Kabul so that I could look for children trying to earn a living on the streets. I gave them money, and if I found that a child's family had no bread-winner to support them I took the child's photo and wrote down their name and address in the hope of finding a sponsor for them in Australia. They, or their mother if she was still alive, could then become part of our sponsorship program. Sponsored widows receive fifty Australian dollars a month and orphans thirty-five Australian dollars a month. It mightn't sound like much, but it's equal to about the average Afghani salary. On the twenty-fifth of every month just after dawn, when the first prayers of the day were over, you could see women coming in their blue *burqas*, with their children, and orphans who had no mother or father. They came from every area of Kabul to Uncle Haji's house in Khair Khana because their families relied on these payments.

The first morning I was out on the streets of Kabul I saw a boy who looked about six and a girl who looked about three picking through a rubbish heap. In Kabul people pile their rubbish in heaps on the footpath – there's usually one heap for every couple of blocks. The children were collect-ing newspapers and any other bits of paper or cardboard they could find and putting them into a big bag. I sat in the car and watched them for a while. The boy picked up a few cherries and raised them to his mouth. Then he looked at the girl, who was looking up at him, and gave her the cherries.

I got out of the car and walked over and asked him, 'Why didn't you eat the cherries?'

He said, 'My sister's looking at me – I had to give them to her.'

'What a wonderful brother you are,' I said. 'Did either of you have breakfast?'

The boy explained that they got up early each morning to collect paper from the rubbish before anyone else had a chance, then they took it home to their mother so she could use it as fuel to burn to make their tea. Breakfast was tea with sugar and a little bit of bread.

The next morning, in another area of Kabul, I saw a little girl and a boy going through rubbish collecting bones and any other food scraps they could find, like onion or potato peelings, and placing them in a bag. I went over and spoke with them. They were cousins, and they collected the scraps for their mothers, who washed them and cooked them up into a soup because they had no money to buy food. Both of them had lost their fathers.

I remember another little boy, about five years old, who was walking around begging, wearing only one sandal – he was carrying the other one because it had fallen apart. It looked to me like it was beyond repair, but he said that he was going to sew it up when he got home. He didn't have any money and couldn't buy another pair of shoes. I said, 'If

I give you enough money to buy a nice pair of shoes, will you do that for me?' He promised me he would, so I gave him some money. I watched him waving goodbye to me as our car drove down the road. I could hear him calling out, 'Thank you, Auntie, thank you, Auntie.'

Later that day I was in a nearby suburb and I heard a voice calling, 'Auntie! Auntie!' I looked around and saw the same boy, still walking with only one sandal on. I said, 'What about the shoes? You promised me you'd buy new shoes.' He told me he would have to buy the shoes later because he was too busy now: he couldn't afford to miss a day's begging because then he and his family wouldn't be able to eat. I made him promise that not only would he go and buy some shoes later with the money I'd given him but that he'd come and see me the next day and show them to me – I was so happy when he turned up at the office proudly wearing his new shoes.

Within a few days I had met fifty children on the street who I had to find Australian sponsors for. I had to stop going out looking for children after that because I wasn't sure I could find enough sponsors to support them all. I didn't want to make promises to them that I mightn't be able to keep. It was upsetting because there were hundreds and hundreds more children on the streets of Kabul just as badly off. I had only reached a handful of them.

~

One day during the second week of my trip I was driving

with Uncle Haji from his house to the orphanage and, passing through an area that had been just empty land when I was a child, I looked out the window and saw rows and rows of shabby tents. It was like Jalozai refugee camp in Peshawar. I was shocked. I said to my uncle, 'I didn't know that in Kabul there were people living in tents.'

He said, 'So many refugees have returned from Pakistan and Iran because they think Kabul is okay, but then they find that their houses have been destroyed.' Tents had started to spring up in the dust on this site about two and a half years earlier and the slum city had continued to grow, until there were over a hundred and fifty families living here. Some of the tents had the logos of international aid agencies on them, but it certainly didn't look like the people were receiving any other aid. I asked my uncle if we could stop the car and go and speak with some of the people living there.

We got out of the car and walked over to the camp. I saw a woman sewing up her tent and asked her what had happened to it. She said it was so windy that every day the tent ripped open and dust blew inside; she had to mend it over and over again. She smiled and said, 'Would you like to come in?' I went inside the tent and felt sad when I saw the conditions she and her family were living in. They had almost nothing except this patch of dust and this torn tent, but she still showed me incredible generosity and hospitality. She made me a cup of tea and handed it to me. I couldn't bring myself to drink from the cup: it was so dirty it looked like it had never been washed. I pointed to my water bottle and said I'd just had a drink and wasn't thirsty, and gave the cup of tea to the woman's little girl, who was sitting beside me. Soon, people from other tents realised that there was a stranger visiting the camp – I could hear them gathering in front of the tent. I went outside and saw twenty or thirty people, including lots of children. They all wanted to tell me about the conditions they were living in.

There was no electricity. They had to walk to collect water. Worst of all, there were no toilets, so people just went behind their tents. Diseases spread quickly, especially amongst the children. The mothers said that children got sick with diarrhoea all the time and some even died. Many of the children were covered in dreadful sores, and hadn't been bathed in weeks. Their hair stood up in spikes, like teenagers in Australia who put gel in their hair to look like punks – except the hair of these children was sticking up because it was full of grease and dirt. The camp was far from the nearest public school so the children just hung around the tents all day.

I spent a couple of hours in the camp talking to people, and then I came back the next day, and every day for a week. I got to know many of the people. Everyone in the camp was living in desperate conditions, but the widows and orphans were the worst off. At night when I lay down I couldn't get to sleep. I kept thinking about them. It was summer and it was unbearably hot in the tents during the day, but when winter came and it started to snow it would be so cold that many of them would freeze to death. I couldn't stand it: we had to find these people somewhere to live.

The next morning I spoke to Uncle Haji about it and he said it was too big a job for us – there must have been at least a thousand people in the tent city. Mahboba's Promise couldn't afford to move them all; it was a job for a big organisation. He stressed that we had only just opened the orphanage and there was a lot of work to be done. He was right.

I said to him, 'How about we try to find somewhere to move a few of the worst-off families, especially the ones who have disabilities from the war and can't earn a living?'

Uncle Haji said, 'Okay, if you can find somewhere for them to stay, we'll help them move.'

I started looking for a big house. I looked at so many houses, talked to so many landlords, but I couldn't find a house that we could afford. Because most of the buildings in Kabul were destroyed by bombs and rockets the rents are extremely high. They've been likened to the rents in Manhattan. For a month's rent on a four-bedroom house landlords were asking up to five hundred US dollars, which is around the average annual salary in Afghanistan.

I had been invited to attend a meeting with representatives from three small Afghani NGOs. After the meeting I went to see some of the widows and children that one of the NGOs was helping. I started speaking to a woman who worked there named Mariam, and began to tell her about the people I had met in the tent city. I said, 'There are aid agencies with billions of dollars in Afghanistan now – why aren't they helping these people? Why is nobody saving the children at least? I don't know what to do.' I burst out crying.

Mariam took hold of my hand. She said, 'There are not many people in Afghanistan crying for others. Come with me.'

She took me outside and pointed to a big two-storey office block next door. It had been built for the Red Crescent, the arm of the Red Cross that operates in Muslim countries, using money donated by the government of the United Arab Emirates. Mariam knew someone high up in the government's planning department and said she would take me to meet him the following morning – perhaps he could help me get part of the building to house people from the tent city. She said, 'But first you'd better see if you like the building or not,' and showed me around. I started to get excited: it was a good, solid building with modern toilets and showers, big windows, and plenty of grass and big trees around it. All it needed was to have kitchens built, electricity connected and carpet and furnishings put in. Many families could live in it very comfortably.

The next day I went and met the man at the planning department. He said, 'What can I do for you?' and I came straight out and said that I wanted Mahboba's Promise to have the building rent-free to house some of the worst-off families from the tent city. He looked amazed that someone would even suggest that. The building was in excellent condition and could have attracted huge rents if it were privately owned. He said, 'You want to have this building for free?'

I said yes, and started telling him about what I had seen in the camp: a man nearly going crazy with grief because he had lost his arms and couldn't support his family, a little girl who had lost her legs from a landmine and was living in a tent in the dust, tiny children starving because no-one could afford to buy them food. 'Somebody has to save them, in the name of God. If the big aid agencies can't do anything, can you do something to help save these people?' I talked and talked and talked until he realised I wasn't going to take no for an answer. He asked me to come the next day to see the head of the Red Crescent.

The man from the planning department came to the meeting and showed his support for my idea, and the head of the Red Crescent agreed to give Mahboba's Promise half of the building rent-free for a year, with water and electricity included for free as well. We wouldn't be able to move people into the building straight away because it has not yet been officially handed over to us, it still needed some final work, and Mahboba's Promise would have to raise money to furnish our section of the building. But at least now the people living in the tents would have something to hope for. The building would come to be known as Hope House.

∼

After *Australian Story* had aired I sent a tape of the program to Kabul, and people passed it around to their friends and family. One man, named Mir Vais, watched the video and decided that I was the woman he wanted to marry. He, his mother, one of his brothers and his brother's wife went to see my Uncle Haji to propose to me.

It wasn't the first proposal I'd received since my divorce. In fact, I'd had more proposals since my divorce than when I was a young girl. When I started going out speaking in public about Mahboba's Promise people heard about me and saw me, and I started receiving proposals from Muslim families who wanted to arrange marriages for their sons. A few non-Muslim Australian men also proposed.

I was happy with my single life, and very busy. I wasn't sure if I could trust a man again and let him into my life. I turned down all the proposals I received, including the one from Mir Vais. He was determined, though. He and his family came to Uncle Haji's house every couple of weeks to propose. I kept telling Uncle Haji to say no. I hadn't given the proposal any thought during my second stay in Kabul, then about a week before I was due to fly back to Australia I came home to Uncle Haji's house one afternoon to find that Mir Vais's mother and sister-in-law had come to propose again – they had heard that I was in Kabul. They told me that Mir Vais really wanted to marry me. 'He's a good man,' Mir Vais's mother said. 'He will look after your children.'

'I'm a busy woman, though,' I said. 'I hardly have time to brush my hair. It would be better for him if he married someone else.'

'Can you at least meet him, just once?'

'I'm sorry, I don't want to get married,' I said. I changed the conversation, telling them about the people I had met in the tents. We chatted for a while. I particularly enjoyed talking with Mir Vais's mother – a gentle, calm woman, she was very easy to talk to and reminded me of my own mother.

Early the next morning, they came to Uncle Haji's house again, and told me that Mir Vais had been up all night praying because I had rejected his proposal. Mir Vais's mother said, 'Please, meet him just once, tonight. If you don't like him, we'll go and won't come back any more.'

That night, Mir Vais, his mother, his brother and sister-in-law came over. I had agreed to meet Mir Vais for the benefit of his mother, not with a view to marrying him, so I didn't have any make-up on, and I was wearing a plain, long black cotton dress with long sleeves and a very simple headscarf. I sat down with Mir Vais and his family in the living room and drank some tea and chatted. We didn't talk about marriage – we spoke mostly about politics and the situation of children in Afghanistan. I had been able to tell as soon as he walked in the room that Mir Vais was a good man. He had innocent eyes and seemed like a spiritual kind of person. He was shy, gentle and polite.

After five minutes or so I excused myself and went upstairs to speak with my Aunt Rona. I said, 'Please go down and ask them not to come proposing to me any more. He is a very nice, honest man but I don't want to get married.' She went downstairs and passed on my message. As the family were leaving, Mir Vais turned and asked Uncle Haji to ask me to do just one thing: perform *Isthikhara* that night. *Isthikhara* is a prayer for guidance that you do when you have a big decision to make. You follow the words of the prayer and ask God which option is best. There are several different traditions for interpreting the answer to your prayers. In my tradition, you go to sleep after praying and wait for the answer to come to you in your dream. Usually you don't know the answer straight away but need to do *Isthikhara* each night for seven nights.

Of course I was not in love with Mir Vais – he was a stranger to me – but I liked his personality and his honesty. I decided that I would leave the decision in God's hands and do *Isthikhara*. I was more spiritual now than I had been the first time I married. This time I would make my decision based upon my religion and my traditions.

I had received a proposal from another man before I left for Afghanistan. I said the *Isthikhara* prayer, asking God if I should marry this other man or Mir Vais. I closed my eyes, fell asleep and that night dreamt of Mir Vais. I saw him playing with Tamana and Sourosh, and talking with my brothers. He looked comfortable and happy in my home with my family. I woke up with a beautiful feeling of calmness and peace.

Mir Vais's sister-in-law came the next day to find out how the *Isthikhara* went. I told her that the answer had been 'yes' but that I still had lots of questions to ask Mir Vais, lots of things to sort out.

Mir Vais called me on my mobile that night, and I asked him many questions to get a better idea of what kind of a husband he would be. I told him that the most important thing to me was my children. Especially since my break-up we had become very close. I told Mir Vais that if I were to marry I didn't want any disruption to Tamana and Sourosh's routine. I didn't want my marriage to make them unhappy for one second. 'Their happiness is my happiness; their sadness is my sadness,' I said.

He told me that he loved children. 'I mightn't be able to be a father to Tamana and Sourosh, but I will try to be a best friend,' he said.

I told him that any husband I had in the future could not try to stop me from doing my work. He assured me that he supported the fact that I was doing work to help widows and orphans – after all, it was seeing my work on *Australian Story* that had made him want to marry me in the first place. Mir Vais himself supported orphans from the village where he was born and lived with his family when he was young.

I said to him: 'I work all the time. Sometimes I come home at twelve o'clock at night. I wouldn't always be able to have dinner on the table. As an Afghani man, how do you feel about that?'

He said, 'It's okay. I'm one of seven brothers, I don't have any sisters, so I'm used to doing housework. I don't want you to change. I hate it when women make themselves slaves of men. You make sacrifices for your orphans and widows; I'll make sacrifices for you.'

He sounded almost too good to be true, but from the direct, down-to-earth way he spoke I could tell he was an honest man. I had always liked the honesty of village men. By doing *Isthikhara* I had already made my decision with

God – my conversation with Mir Vais confirmed it and reassured me that he was a good man. I was going to marry him.

Two nights later, we had an engagement party with about thirty guests. I bought some pink material and took it to a tailor to make an outfit, but I was too busy at the tent city to have a fitting so it was a little big for me. For most of the engagement party the women and men celebrated in separate rooms. Uncle Haji handed over a tray of sweets, which officially signified my acceptance of Mir Vais's proposal, and at that point I began to cry in front of Mir Vais's female relatives. I was thinking of Tamana and Sourosh, and how they would have to face another challenge when Mir Vais came to live with us. It would be a big change for them to get used to. I was also emotional because I was facing a new chapter in my life and I didn't know how it was going to turn out.

Later, Mir Vais was brought in so that he could put an engagement ring on my finger. He looked handsome in a white Afghani *shalwar kameez* and a black vest. He stood beside me, holding my hand, as everyone danced around us. The one thing that made me feel less uncertain about the future was seeing the extent of his happiness. He was over the moon. He showed no doubts or second thoughts. He was overjoyed and constantly thanking God that I had said yes to him. And when you see someone that happy, you're happy, too.

We had to be married in only two days' time to fit in with my flight back to Australia. Mir Vais's father, who was living and working in Dubai, sent us over some money to pay for a wedding reception. Most of the venues were already booked, but we managed to find a small, inexpensive place, the Ariana Hotel, where we could hold the wedding and lunch afterwards. Everyone in our families pitched in to help prepare for the wedding and invite people. In Afghanistan people don't usually make a fuss about a remarriage but Mir Vais's family made me feel as special as if I were a young girl being married for the first time. We got everything done so smoothly and quickly it was as if the angels had come down from the sky to help us.

I was also busy over at the tent city, interviewing people so that I could choose the most disadvantaged families to be moved into Hope House when it became available. Once I had identified who needed housing the most urgently I recorded their names on a list. Mir Vais came to the tent city several times in those days and helped me. I was impressed with the way he attended to the children, especially the orphans. He was patient with them, and patient with the work that I was doing. He didn't mind me talking to male strangers as part of my work, while many men wouldn't have wanted me to. He showed his support and commitment by promising to do volunteer work in Kabul for Mahboba's Promise until he was able to join me in Australia.

On the morning of our wedding day I was at the tent city finishing off my interviews when he called me on my mobile. We had arranged that he would pick up my wedding dress for me from the tailor but the tailor had said Mir Vais couldn't take it because I had to try it on first. I told Mir Vais where I was, and instead of being annoyed that I was working on our wedding day he laughed. He picked me up and took me to the tailor and then to the beautician to have my make-up done. There was no reason this time not to make myself look pretty. This time there would be no sadness associated with my wedding – it would be a celebration.

I wore a long dark-green dress that was overlaid with beautiful green lace. There had been no time to have a white bridal dress made for me to change into after the ceremony, but I did get to wear a white veil, just as I had always dreamed of. By Afghani standards our wedding was small. The sheikh came and performed the ceremony at the hotel and afterwards lunch was served to about two hundred guests. We'd only had a couple of days to organise invitations but in Afghanistan it isn't hard to get people to come to a wedding.

I had not planned to come back from my trip to Afghanistan a married woman. Everything had happened so fast that on my wedding day I felt sort of numb. But I was happy, too, because Mir Vais made it clear that he appreciated me for who I was and didn't want to try and change me or the way I lived my life. It made me happy to know that someone was so happy to have me.

The wedding was hardly over before I had to pack my bags and head home to Australia. We gave our wedding gifts to the orphans. All I brought home from my trip was my wedding dress. Mir Vais was terribly upset at the airport, but I was happy because I had missed Tamana and Sourosh and knew I would be seeing them soon. I told Mir Vais that our separation wouldn't be forever. I would be returning to Afghanistan as soon as I had raised the money we needed to open Hope House – and once his visa application had been approved he would eventually be able to join his new family in Australia.

# Chapter 17

Sometimes when I look back over my life I can hardly believe where I am today. I remember myself as a teenage girl in Peshawar scrubbing clothes, dreaming about one day being in charge of distributing aid to people. When I had the chance I would do things differently. I would put the aid straight into the hands of the people who needed it; I would go to the root, not the top of the tree. And now that's what I'm doing.

The medical centre and girls school in Abdara opened in 2003. We had intended it to be a women's medical centre but men turned up for treatment, too. There were no medical services at all in Abdara, so we couldn't refuse them. Five of the villagers had heart problems and had travelled to Kabul to see doctors, who had said there was nothing they could do for them; they would eventually die.

Our doctor gave these patients some medication that had been donated in Australia – and the drugs controlled their heart symptoms. There were many arthritis sufferers in the village and the doctor gave them a liniment to rub on their joints, something like Deep Heat. It mightn't sound like much, but they didn't have anything like that in Abdara, and when they rubbed it on they felt their pain ease and their joints start to feel less stiff.

The patients believed that God was working through the medical centre. Word spread to neighbouring villages and people began travelling from all over the area to come and receive treatment; some even walked past much closer medical centres to come to see our doctor. Pretty soon, people were queuing up. Sometimes, by 5 am there were three hundred people waiting for the doctor.

The school is open to girls aged between seven and thirteen. It was winter and snow was starting to fall when the school was ready to open. Schools normally close in that part of Afghanistan over winter but I asked Uncle Haji to open it straight away rather than waste three months. Because girls had never received an education in Abdara before, on the first day only twenty girls turned up.

The volunteer group Wrap with Love, who make blankets to bring warmth and comfort to disadvantaged people around the world, had donated two hundred blankets to Mahboba's Promise. I had sent them over to Uncle Haji and on that first school day he gave each of the girls a blanket. They were colourful, some were decorated with flowers, and they were very warm. According to Uncle

Haji those blankets worked like magic. The next day, after the rest of the village had seen the girls walking home wrapped in their beautiful warm blankets, a hundred and thirty girls turned up for school. Uncle Haji asked me to pass on a big thank-you to the volunteers who knitted those blankets, because they made his job so much easier.

Uncle Haji had been very frustrated during the construction of the buildings. It had caused him a lot of headaches. Once it was finished he had said to me, 'No more construction in Panjshir Valley, this is the first and the last.' But then one day he had to go to Abdara to distribute some clothing donated in Australia to some widows there. He hired a big van to transport lots of heavy bags of warm clothes, but would need help once he got to Panjshir Valley to carry the bags inside so that the widows could come and collect the clothes. It was snowing. He went to the school and asked the girls if they would help him. Within twenty minutes they had moved everything from the van into one of the school rooms. He told me that he had never enjoyed being with a group of children so much in all his life. When he saw these girls wrapped in their colourful blankets, chatting and laughing their way through the job, he knew that building the school had been worth all the trouble and more.

My mother cried with happiness when I showed her videos and photos of the girls going to school, and people lining up for treatment at the medical centre. To my father, who has a strong connection to Abdara through his own father, it is one of the best projects I have ever been involved in.

The widow and orphan sponsorship program continues, and has been expanded through the Kabul Outreach Program, which was started by my husband, Mir Vais, and another volunteer. The program involves volunteers going out and talking to street children and widows who are too proud to come forward and ask for help. Another important part of the program is going out to check that the widows and orphans who are receiving sponsorship money are truly in need and are not receiving other incomes. We support around three hundred and twenty widows and orphans each month in Kabul.

Fifty-three widows and children are living in Hope House. We have moved the sewing machines there from Uncle Haji's house so the women and girls can learn to sew. We have employed a man to live at Hope House to cook food for the widows and children and teach them how to speak English. He is an experienced shoemaker and is training some of the boys in shoemaking. We have employed a sewing teacher and a tutor to help the children with their homework and teach them religious studies; the children go to a nearby public school.

It wasn't easy to get Hope House open. It took time to raise enough money to furnish the building, but that was only part of the delay. In Afghanistan bureaucracy moves very slowly and delays of six months to a year are quite common. After waiting about five months I flew to Kabul again in January 2004 to finally open Hope House. When I got to the tent city I was devastated to find out that an eighteen-year-old girl who was on the list to move into

Hope House had killed herself. Her mother said she had been depressed for months about being stuck in the camp, and had begun to think that my promises to move people from the tents were empty. The girl's mother, and her two brothers and one sister, were among the first to be moved from their tent, but I will never forget the girl and the pointless loss of her life.

When I went back to the camp to collect the families and take them to Hope House it was a chaotic scene, with parents and children all gathering around me, overjoyed that they were finally leaving. I noticed an old woman walking around aimlessly, separate from the crowd. She was crying and beating herself on the head with her fists. She was black with dirt, her hair was matted and she was wearing a filthy dress. A little girl who looked about six was following her, barefoot. I went over and asked the old woman what the matter was. She answered me in a language I didn't understand, but the little girl introduced herself in Dari as Masuda and told me that this was her grandmother. She'd had five children but they were dead. All the family she had left was her stepson and her granddaughter, Masuda. Afghanistan is one of the world's biggest producers of opium poppies and heroin addiction is becoming a major problem: the old woman's stepson was an addict and had been beating her, and now had kicked both her and Masuda out of the tent.

The old woman was yelling something and I asked Masuda what she was saying. 'My grandma's saying, "Where will we go now? Where will we go now?"' she said.

I grabbed the old woman's hand and said, 'I'll take you to Hope House, that's why I'm here.'

That old woman will always stay in my heart because it seemed like a miracle that at the moment she needed somebody I happened to be there. I took her and Masuda to the *hamam* before taking them to Hope House, because they hadn't been able to bathe for nine months. The attendant was worried about letting them in because they were so dirty they might spread germs to other people but I said, 'I'm paying you, you have to accept them.' I paid one of the staff to scrub the old woman but it was such a big job that she started to get tired so I took over. I had to wash her hair thirteen times before it was clean. Everybody in the *hamam* was staring at us. I said, 'This is my Mama.'

They said, 'Oh, she is not your Mama, you found her in some corner of a camp.'

I said, 'No, this is my Mama,' and held her close to me.

Now my Mama is living in Hope House with Masuda. She doesn't have to worry about food or housing any more, and as the oldest woman in Hope House she enjoys the respect of everyone.

Forty-eight children are living in the orphanage in Uncle Haji's old house in Kabul. They go to a nearby public school, and because they also have a tutor to help them at home most of them are a year ahead of other children their age at school. In 2004 we took over the care of sixty-nine boys whose parents were killed in an earthquake in Afghanistan in 1998. A kind Afghani man had taken them to the Jalozai refugee camp in Peshawar, but they had no means of support and had no choice but to beg. Now we send them an allowance each month so they don't have to beg, and we have started giving them an education. In Uncle Haji's and my eyes, once children have food the next most urgent thing to give them is education.

All of our schools remain open, and the classrooms are always full to capacity. There are still not enough schools in Afghanistan and the refugee camps of Pakistan, and children are thirsty for education. Even if you set up a blackboard outside you will get a hundred children coming to sit in the dust to learn. Only one in three Afghani adults can read and write, and only one in five women. I am counting on the children in our schools. I'm counting on every one of them to become somebody useful in their community so that they can help to rebuild Afghanistan.

I have been developing a Sister School Program in which a school in Australia is partnered with one in Afghanistan. Students at one school which has been involved in the program, Asquith Girls High in Sydney, have raised money to help the students at the Abdara Girls School in Panjshir Valley, buying things such as an electricity generator, shoes for all the girls and a camera. The students here and at Abdara send each other letters and photos to get to know each other. The Australian kids learn to appreciate what they have, and the importance of helping others. They come to understand that it is possible to have love for all human beings no matter what their religion or cultural background. I believe that what children need more than anything else in their lives is peace, and peace won't come from guns or money. The only way to create peace is through love, care and understanding. I hope that by building friendship between children from two different worlds the Sister School Program will help to create a more peaceful world in the future.

The work Dr Nasrin started in Peshawar continues, although Dr Nasrin herself has had to reduce her involvement after starting a family. Her sister Hawa and niece Brishna now do the majority of the work, with help from Dr Nasrin and other family members. Many refugees have returned to Afghanistan from Peshawar, easing the pressure. Still, each month they give ten widows a monthly allowance and pay the school fees of twenty-five orphans.

Uncle Haji and Aunt Rona remain in Kabul. Uncle Haji's life is totally committed to helping the children of Afghanistan. He is getting older and tireder, and is now focusing his energy on the orphanage in Shahr-e-now. His goal is to bring up the children there to be good people, to help them create a positive, secure future for themselves.

Together we have achieved an incredible amount. When I speak to other NGOs in Afghanistan they find it hard to believe how much we've managed to do in such a short time and with only a small budget. But we have the advantage of understanding the country and the way it works, the language and the culture. We know people who will donate goods and services to us. We know what the right price is so we don't get overcharged. And we know about remote areas where help is desperately needed, while people from overseas may not.

Despite what we've achieved, sometimes I start to panic about the future. Thousands of women and children are depending upon us every day. If I am one day late in sending money over to Pakistan or Afghanistan hundreds of families will go a day without food. It's like having a huge extended family. I still worry about the remaining people in the tent city in Kabul, but we would need more funds to move more families into Hope House. The medical centre in Abdara has had an enormous impact on the people in Panjshir Valley, but it is very expensive to run. The committee members and I have discussed forming relationships with other NGOs so that we can keep growing and helping more people. There are several big aid organisations that have money and want to help but don't have the background knowledge and contacts that we do, and hopefully in the future we will be able to work together.

We have already formed a relationship with Muslim Aid Australia, who help support our medical centre in Abdara, our widow and orphan sponsorship program, and schools in Jalozai refugee camp in Peshawar. They also pay for our Feed the Fasting program during Ramadan each year. For the whole of the month of Ramadan people are not to eat or drink from sunrise till sunset. It is a very hard time for the poor because they go all day without food and become weak – then have nothing to feed themselves with at night. Ramadan is also a time of helping out those in need. During the month, Uncle Haji in Kabul and Dr Nasrin in Peshawar provide a meal each evening for the poor.

Here in Australia we continue to work out of my garage. Every day of the week some of my twenty or so volunteers come to help run the office and raise money. I have been blessed to have very intelligent and hard-working people come to help out – most of them have demanding jobs themselves. They have helped turn me from a woman who had stacks of letters and documents piled up on her dining table into one who now has the basic office systems in place. My friend and very dedicated volunteer Gill has a university degree in business adminis-tration and has run her own business for years. When she first heard of the work I was doing and came to help in 2003 she could see what changes needed to be made for things to run more smoothly. She helped me and the organisation develop a computer database linking sponsors and their sponsored widows and orphans, and also helped to streamline our bookkeeping. She, like all of my volunteers, has made sacrifices in her life to help other people. Sometimes Gill doesn't leave my office until one in the morning.

One of the strengths of Mahboba's Promise is that anyone is welcome to volunteer so long as they have a good heart. My door is open to everyone. I have Hindu, Christ-ian, Buddhist, Muslim, Catholic, Chinese, Indian, Fijian and Aussie volunteers, and more. I love them all, and I've learnt something from every one of them. When they come to my house to work in the garage I try to show them love and respect; I give them something to eat or a cup of tea. They're my family, too.

~

My mother lives in Blacktown, in Sydney. The years since she moved to Australia have been the best of her life. The worries she had when her children were spread across the world, living as refugees, are over. The hardships of her life in Kabul are all behind her. She doesn't have to worry about anything any more. She gets lonely sometimes because she has never managed to learn English, but three of my brothers live close by, and we all visit and call her as often as we can. I don't think there's anything I can say about my mother that will ever communicate how much I love her – for her sacrifices, for her kindness, for being available to me and my brothers and sisters day or night when we're sick, when we're happy, when we're not happy. She has always loved each one of her nine children the same and has spent all of her time and energy – all of her life – raising us.

My father lives in Brisbane with his wife, Nadira. They migrated to Australia a few years after my mother and younger brothers and sister. They now have four sons and three daughters, who I love like my other brothers and sisters. Earlier in my life, there were years at a time when I had very little contact with my father, but now I have a good relationship with him, my stepmother and my half brothers and sisters. I call him regularly and visit him in Brisbane when I get a chance. He is in his mid-seventies and is retired, but still very busy. He has filled his front and back yard with flowerbeds and sells flowers on Sundays at a market in Brisbane. He saves up the money and sends it to needy people he knows of in Afghanistan, and has helped several of them buy shops and start their own small businesses.

I owe my mother and father everything because if they hadn't raised me the way they did, teaching me to be independent and strong, I wouldn't have survived the walk to Peshawar, or living as a refugee. And I would have crumbled without a husband to look after me. I wouldn't be the person I am today.

Omar and his wife and children recently moved back to Sydney after living in Perth for several years; they are now living in Blacktown. When he first came to Australia Omar did a sociology degree at the University of New South Wales. He wanted to create opportunities for my brothers so he set up a family business, a shop in Auburn, Sydney, called the Afghan Market, specialising in Afghani groceries, and all my brothers have worked there at some time.

Omar has been not only a brother to me but a friend and a father figure as well; he has played a huge part in my life. He has sacrificed himself for me and my brothers and sisters ever since he was a teenager, putting our needs before his own. He has helped me understand myself and the world around me.

Anwar lives in Brisbane now – he moved there with his wife and children because he wanted to buy a nice house for them, and Brisbane was more affordable. He has worked as a taxi driver but he really has a business mind – he ran the Afghan Market for a time – and would like to start another business. Early on, Anwar gave up much of his own life to look after me, and we are still close. When we get together we are like old friends talking about old times, like when we had no money to buy food in India.

My third eldest brother, Assad, lives in Brisbane with his wife and children. He has learnt a lot of skills so far in his life: he is a mechanic and can fix any problem with a car and he is a very good handyman. He did the fit-out for the Afghan Market.

My relationships with all of my brothers and sisters are very strong, but I think my bond with Zarmina, my sister who is two years younger than me, is the strongest. She's my best friend, the person I call when I'm crying in the middle of the night. When Zarmina came to Australia she learnt English and went to TAFE to do some courses. She married one of our cousins and they live in Harris Park, in Sydney, and have started a family. She is still the giving person she was when we were girls, helping out when any of us is sick or worried about something.

Yama and Abdullah, who are only two years apart, are very close to each other. They run the Afghan Market together and have also bought a house together, in Blacktown. Yama and Abdullah are both married with children. Both families live happily together in the same house, and Yama and Abdullah share the profits of the business and the expenses of the household as though they were one family. Yama studied pathology and worked at Sydney's Royal North Shore Hospital for a while, but prefers working in the family business. He is the more serious, business-minded of the two.

Abdullah is both the quietest and the funniest member of the family. Whenever he's around you can't help but be happy. Even from negative situations he manages to find humour.

My brother Sidiq is a little bit like my father – quite commanding but kind and soft-hearted. In 2004 I learnt of a group of orphans in the slums of Shakerdara, in Kabul, who had built their own one-room homes out of mud but were looking for money to put roofs on them. I made urgent phone calls to some of my donors in Australia and raised $7,000 in a few days. Uncle Haji already had too much work to do so Sidiq travelled to Kabul to oversee the building of the roofs, but when he got there he found that the houses were just mud huts that would probably be washed away at the first sign of rain. Australian dollars go a long way in Afghanistan and he could afford to have them knocked down and new shelters built. Sidiq stayed in Kabul for three months until the job was done, separated from his wife and three children, and his business. He said, 'What job is better than the job of looking after others?' I always knew that he was a kind man, a caring husband and a good father to his children, but until then I didn't realise the extent of his selflessness. I believe that he may be on the way to becoming a new driving force for Mahboba's Promise in Afghanistan, alongside Uncle Haji.

My youngest sister, Zargona, did a pharmacy degree in Australia and is working at Westmead Hospital in Sydney as a pharmacist. Although we didn't get to spend much time together when we were young because I went to Peshawar, she is a very special part of my life. There was so much sadness and fear in Kabul when she was a baby, but looking after her, seeing her first smiles and attempts at walking and talking, brought me a lot of happiness and laughter. She is now married and starting a family.

My first husband, Assad, got married to a woman from Afghanistan and they have a child. Assad sees Tamana and Sourosh every week. I wish Assad happiness in his life. I always pray that he finds the peace that I have found and that he will have a good life with his new wife.

At the end of 2004 my husband, Mir Vais, moved to live with me in Australia. Although it was a challenge at first for Tamana and Sourosh to have someone new come into the family, they are developing a good relationship. Mir Vais has kept his promise not to disrupt the routine that I had with the children, and he shows them unconditional love and attention every day. He always has a smile for them, or a story to tell them. He would do anything to make them happy.

I am thankful that Mir Vais has given his total support to my work. There have been times when I have been so busy with work and driving the kids to and from school that I couldn't even think about doing housework, but when I get home the house is spotless, thanks to Mir Vais. He is patient with the fact that when I am very busy he hardly sees me, that our home is an office, that people ring day and night, and that there are always volunteers and committee members coming and going. Unlike some Afghani husbands, I don't need to seek his permission to go out to give talks or go to fundraising events, because he trusts me and accepts me for who I am.

Mir Vais is doing English classes three days a week and is working towards becoming a bricklayer – which he was trained to be in Afghanistan – when his English has improved. There are times when he misses his mother and brothers desperately, but he is happy that he made the decision to join me and start a new life in Australia. We share the same beliefs. Both of us value honesty in a relationship and feel that it is important to express our feelings, not keep things bottled up. I am lucky to have him as a husband. I have always believed that good things happen when you do good for others – it is as though marrying Mir Vais is a reward for the work that I have done.

Tamana and Sourosh are a loving sister and brother, and they don't fight as much as many other brothers and sisters. Sourosh looks up to Tamana with respect, and Tamana looks out for Sourosh almost like a mother.

Tamana plans to finish year ten and then have a year's break from study, get a job and decide what further study she would like to do. She is excellent with children – she is patient and understands how to deal with them – and she plans to one day open and run her own childcare centre. Tamana means more to me than she can ever know; I feel a special love and pride for my daughter. She and I have been through so much sadness and joy together that it hurts me to spend even one night apart from her.

Sourosh is a mature little boy with a wide general knowledge – he can talk about anything. He is spiritual and loves to study religion, and is also interested in politics. He is very humane, always thinking about poor people. He argues against injustice and war. He has big dreams for the future – he wants to study law and become someone who can make a difference. While I focus on the people of Afghanistan he thinks about the global picture, about poverty and injustice all over the world.

Through being exposed to my work Tamana and Sourosh have learnt an important lesson: to care for others. They give their own clothes and toys to the orphans; they drop any spare coins they have into a donation tin. I have tried to teach them to appreciate what they have and be good to others. If they have learnt this, no matter what they do after they finish school, they will be good people.

~

Since I started raising money to send over to Afghanistan and Pakistan my whole attitude to money has changed. To me it just looks like pieces of paper. Even if someone gave me a million dollars and said, 'You have to keep this million dollars, you can't give it away,' it would just be a million pieces of paper. The only value money has to me any more is in saving lives. Apart from paying the rent and buying food and clothes and the things my family needs, I don't need money. Some people think that's crazy and that life is better when you have lots of money. But money buys you nothing unless you know the meaning of happiness within yourself.

My life is worth more now than it ever has been. I was passing time before. I feel bad when I think about how many people were dying while I was busy buying furniture and jewellery and a car, and thinking about buying a house. That was always my dream before Mahboba's Promise started: to own a house in Australia. That dream no longer exists. The only dream I have now is to build a beautiful orphanage in Kabul big enough to house two hundred children.

I can see it clearly in my mind. It is a huge building with many bedrooms filled with beds like we have in Australia and comfortable pillows, colourful blankets and Persian rugs covering the floor. There's one big open room where once a week the children can come to do whatever they like: paint, draw, shout, scream, dance. The orphans of Kabul are always very disciplined because they've had to grow up too fast; they don't have the luxury of being able to play around or do anything silly. They are careful not to drop anything or make anything dirty. I want them to have the opportunity to let go and have fun like other kids. Once a week they will be able to go into this big room and do whatever they like, and someone will clean up later.

Right next to the dormitory is a primary school and a high school, and next to that there's a small medical centre with a 24-hour emergency room. There are lovely green lawns all around the buildings, and flowerbeds and trees. There's a big oval for the children to play sport on. Buildings in Afghanistan are always surrounded by a tall brick wall, but the orphanage will have a hedge instead. The children won't feel like they're walled in. I will walk every street of Kabul and find orphans who are homeless or working under age and take them to their new home.

Already we have taken the first steps to building this dream. I have been raising money to undertake the first stage of the project, constructing the dormitory, and Sidiq has returned to Afghanistan to find suitable land. There is a desperate need for the new orphanage. The official estimate is that there are over one and a half million orphans in Afghanistan, but I fear that there may be even more because it is hard to keep records. I managed to get the free lease on Hope House extended until 2007 but after that the widows and orphans there will need somewhere else to live. And there is an urgent need for housing for orphans with disabilities. Years of war have left many as amputees, or with other permanent injuries, and for these children it is even harder to survive.

When Sidiq was in Afghanistan helping house the orphans in Shakerdara, he also assisted with the Kabul Outreach Program. He came across a nine-year-old boy who had lost one of his arms to a landmine while collecting wood. His father was dead, so he was begging to support his family. Sidiq arranged for the boy to receive a monthly allowance to live on, but what the boy really wanted – and needed – was to be cared for in an orphanage. There was not enough room for him, and this highlighted to me how quickly we need to get building work under way for the new orphanage. I realised that it was time to really start thinking about the needs of the many disabled orphans in Afghanistan, and so part of the new orphanage will be devoted to disabled children and designed with their needs in mind.

My aim is to raise the children in the orphanage into adults who can help build the future Afghanistan. I don't want them to lose their Afghani traditions; I want them to appreciate and maintain their Afghani culture. I don't want to Westernise them, but rather I want them to be able to compete in the modern Western world, with a good understanding of the standard school subjects but also computer skills, general knowledge of world politics, and English and Arabic as well as the two main Afghani languages, Pashto and Dari. I would like to employ someone to give the children spiritual guidance, because I want them to find spiritual peace. When you truly find spritiual peace you cannot harm others. For their physical fitness I would like them all to get involved in sport and exercise. The emotional side of their lives is also important. I am hoping that we will be able to send over Australian volunteers who have experience in counselling and can help them recover from the trauma they have been through.

Education and love are the keys to the successful rebuilding of Afghanistan. Education will give children the skills and knowledge they need to succeed in life. And learning to love other people, regardless of ethnic or religious differences, will bring peace after so many years of war. If I can help at least two hundred children grow up to want peace, perhaps they can show others the way.

I want the children in the new orphanage to have choices. I don't want to tell them what to do with their lives, or make them feel that they owe me something. My aim is to give them education and support so that when they are older they can stand on their own feet, with a world of freedom and choice in front of them. I want to give them opportunities, and they can do whatever they wish with them. There is so much hate and anger in the world, but if you show children love they will choose the right way – the way of love and peace – themselves.

I used to ask myself the question: what's my part in the world? My part is to bring up the lost children of Afghanistan to be loving and peaceful. And they will be an example for all the world to follow.

You can help make a difference to the lives of widows and orphans in Afghanistan – by donating time, money, services or expertise. Even the smallest contribution can change a person's life.

Mahboba's Promise
PO Box 6234
North Ryde NSW 2113

Tel (02) 9887 1665    Fax (02) 9889 0473
Email: mahboba@mahbobaspromise.org
www.mahbobaspromise.org

# Acknowledgments

We would like to thank Tamana, Sourosh and Mir Vais for their patience and kindness during the many months it took to write this book, and Ronnie Gramazio for all his support. Thanks to Zargona Rawi for looking over the spelling of Afghani and Arabic names.

Thanks to Mahboba's Promise volunteers Gill Shadduck and Kate Hodges for giving their time to provide useful background information on the day-to-day operations of the organisation, and to Jenni Priestley. Thanks to friends, volunteers and supporters of Mahboba's Promise whose photos appear in the book.

At Random House, our thanks go to publisher Fiona Henderson and project editor Katie Stackhouse, for their enthusiasm for the project from the beginning, and to Sophie Ambrose and Catherine Hill for reading an early draft and providing invaluable encouragement and suggestions.

Thankyou to copyeditor Jo Jarrah for her thoughtful and sensitive editing and helpful editorial report, proofreader Ella Martin for her care and attention, and to Richard Potter.

And of course, the greatest of thanks to all the volunteers and supporters of Mahboba's Promise.

# Sources

Statistics relating to education, literacy rates, annual average income and the Afghani orphan population were sourced from the most up-to-date statistics available at the time of writing, compiled by:

UNICEF – for more statistics, see *www.unicef.org*

UNESCO – for more statistics, see *www.unesco.org*

**Bibliography**

For clarity on details of Afghanistan's history and the lives of its people we acknowledge the following sources:

*Books and magazines*

Ewans, Martin 2005 *Afghanistan*, HarperCollins, New York.

McKew, Maxine 30/9/03 'Lunch With Maxine McKew: Mahboba Rawi', *The Bulletin*.

*The New Encyclopaedia Britannica* Macropaedia 2003, Encyclopaedia Britannica Inc, Chicago.

Newby, Eric 1981 *A Short Walk in the Hindu Kush*, Picador, London.

Swift Yasgur, Batya 2002 *Behind the Burqa: Our Life in Afghanistan and How We Escaped to Freedom,* John Wiley & Sons, Inc, Hoboken, New Jersey.

Vogelsang, Willem 2002 *The Afghans,* Blackwell Publishers Ltd, Oxford.


*Websites*

Amnesty International's annual reports on Afghanistan 1995–2004: *www.amnesty.org*

Encyclopaedia of the Orient, on LexicOrient: *www.lexicorient.com*

Human Rights Watch: *www.hrw.org*

Integrated Regional Information Networks, part of the UN Office for the Coordination of Humanitarian Affairs: *www.irinnews.org*

*islam.about.com*

Medecins Sans Frontieres/Doctors Without Borders: *www.doctorswithoutborders.org*

National Geographic: *www.nationalgeographic.com*

The Washington Post: *www.washingtonpost.com*